Handbook
APPELLATE ADVOCACY
Second Edition

Prepared By

UCLA MOOT COURT HONORS PROGRAM

Edited By

Frank R. Acuña

Daniel E. Casas

Claire P. McGreal

John Ossiff

Roger M. Rosen

AMERICAN CASEBOOK SERIES

WEST PUBLISHING CO.
ST. PAUL, MINN., 1986

COPYRIGHT © 1967, 1978 UCLA MOOT COURT HONORS PROGRAM
COPYRIGHT © 1980 By WEST PUBLISHING CO.
COPYRIGHT © 1986 By WEST PUBLISHING CO.

50 West Kellogg Boulevard
P.O. Box 64526
St. Paul, Minnesota 55164–0526

All rights reserved
Printed in the United States of America

Library of Congress Cataloging in Publication Data

Handbook of appellate advocacy.

Includes index.
1. Briefs—United States. 2. Oral pleading—United
States. 3. Appellate procedure—United States.
I. Acuna, Frank R. II. UCLA Moot Court Honors Program.
KF251.H36 1986   808'.066347   86–1710

ISBN 0–314–98476–3

Hdbk.App. Advocacy 2nd Ed. ACB

1st Reprint—1987

Preface and Acknowledgements
to the Second Edition

The *Handbook of Appellate Advocacy* has been revised constantly since its 1980 publication date. While much of the original material has been retained, a number of changes have been made as a result of suggestions by students from law schools across the country. The focus of the Second Edition has been shifted exclusively to Moot Court participants. Reference is now made to student briefs in the case of *Vitas v. Younger & Burton.* The Petitioner's brief for this case is included in Appendix A, in its entirety. The Editors thank Valerie Ackerman, Sally Helppie, Susan Keller, and Gina Liudzius for allowing their briefs and oral arguments to be used as examples.

Two stylistic changes have been made throughout this handbook. First, advocacy requires emphasis and directness. Therefore, the passive voice is used only when necessary and unnecessary material, examples, and words were deleted whenever possible. Second, the U.C.L.A. Moot Court Honors Program is committed to eliminating sexism. Therefore, all gender-specific language which does not refer to a particular person was deleted. Additionally, excerpts from "Guidelines for Equal Treatment of the Sexes in McGraw-Hill Book Company Publications" are reproduced in Appendix D.

In addition to those persons involved in preparing previous editions of the handbook, the Editors are indebted to Dean Susan Prager, Associate Dean Carole Goldberg-Ambrose, and Professors Julian Eule and Patrick Patterson of the U.C.L.A. School of Law. Ms. Thelma Dekker and Mr. Arthur King of the law school's word processing staff somehow juggled an impossible workload to complete seemingly endless drafts.

Finally, the entire U.C.L.A. Moot Court Executive Board of Judges willingly helped whenever asked. Of these people, the Editors are particularly indebted to John Moscarino and Robert Noriega for providing necessary resources, and to Susan Abraham, Jeffrey Goldstein, Kathryn Karcher, Brad Krasnoff, James McSpiritt, and Steven Plotkin for proofreading our work.

F.R.A.
D.E.C.
C.P.M.
J.O.
R.M.R.

Los Angeles, California
October, 1985

*

Preface to the First Edition

This handbook is designed to help the beginning appellate advocate—student Moot Court participant and novice attorney alike. Because it is a handbook, certain subjects have been treated in a cursory manner. Throughout the book reference is made to other sources, such as applicable court rules and texts dealing with the specific, discrete elements of a brief.

Because the handbook is designed to assist an advocate who has already decided to file an appeal in his case, rules governing when an appeal may be taken and the various procedural steps necessary to file an appeal are not discussed. Obviously, the initial decision to approach an appellate court determines the tone of the brief, its length, the issues which it emphasizes, and the audience for which it is written. This handbook is designed to assist the inexperienced advocate to write a persuasive brief within this predetermined framework.

The advocate's tools of persuasion are his brief and his oral argument. The importance of each varies substantially from court to court. In some jurisdictions, cases are decided primarily on the briefs with oral argument consisting of little more than a last opportunity to convince the court that it should or should not enter its tentative opinion as a final judgment. For this reason, the basic structure of a brief is carefully reviewed and examples are provided in Chapter One. Chapter Two offers a discussion of the elements of persuasive writing, and the rules governing citation format are detailed in Chapter Three. Some jurisdictions rely heavily upon the face-to-face confrontation of oral argument to set the tone of the case and clarify the main issues prior to any decision. Accordingly, Chapter Four discusses the preparation and presentation of an oral argument.

Throughout the handbook reference is made to the case of *Peggy v. Smith & Jones*. The Petitioner's brief for this case is included as Appendix A. The reader may choose first to read this brief to gain some familiarity with the case as it is used in the examples.

Finally, the advocate should remember that no book can provide the experience necessary for one to become an accomplished advocate. The job of the advocate requires that he be sensitive to every element that may lead to the persuasive quality of his presentation, and experience alone teaches this best. Moot Court provides the student with an opportunity to marshal his talents as an advocate and apply them to a realistic situation. If this opportunity is approached seriously it should be a most valuable experience.

*

Acknowledgement to the First Edition

The Editors are indebted to their colleagues in the UCLA Moot Court Honors Program for assistance and suggestions in the preparation of this work. Robert Dawson and Michael Quesnel generously volunteered their time, energy, and expertise to co-author Chapter Four, "The Oral Presentation," and assisted in numerous other ways. This Handbook is in large part the result of their efforts, for which we are greatly appreciative. Douglas Barnes, Shirley Curfman, Marlene Goodfried, and Thomas Mabie kindly assisted the Editors by proofreading and offering stylistic suggestions.

The Editors wish particularly to thank Ms. Mary Burdick of the Western Center on Law and Poverty and Mr. Kent Richland, clerk for the California Second District Court of Appeal, for editing and suggesting revisions of the text. Their substantive and stylistic additions have greatly enhanced the value of this work.

This Handbook had its genesis in the *Handbook of Appellate Advocacy,* published for the UCLA Moot Court Honors Program in 1969 by Michael Josephson, Kenneth Kleinberg, and Franklin Tom. This Handbook would not exist but for their labors, for which we are grateful.

In addition to those who offered substantive and stylistic suggestions, other individuals merit recognition for their help in this project. Ms. Betty Dirstine and other members of the UCLA Law School secretarial staff patiently typed and revised the numerous drafts of this text, and Ms. Michelle Thrush transcribed the oral argument included in Appendix B to this Handbook.

Many members of the bench and bar, as well as the faculty of the UCLA Law School, gave helpful advice during the various stages of the preparation. Comments and recommendations were solicited from numerous individuals. In particular, we wish to thank Judge Leonard I. Garth, United States Court of Appeal, Third Circuit; Irving R. Kaufman, Chief Judge, United States Court of Appeal, Second Circuit; Harry Phillips, Chief Judge, United States Court of Appeal, Sixth Circuit; Lester Roth, Presiding Justice, California Court of Appeal, Second District; Judge Robert S. Thompson, California Court of Appeal, Second District; Ellis Horvitz; and Michael Josephson.

Finally, we wish to think Professors Paul Boland, Gail Kass, and Randy Vassar, who generously provided their time and expertise throughout the course of the project.

The Editors wish to note that the pronoun "he" is used throughout the handbook as a matter of convenience. Unfortunately, no widely accepted and stylistically satisfactory pronoun has yet been devised to represent advocates—men and women alike. Whenever particular reference is made to counsel for Petitioner in the case of *Peggy v. Smith & Jones,* the pronoun "she" is used since the brief for *Peggy v. Smith & Jones* was prepared and argued by Gwen Whitson and Kathy Rohwer.

B.E.D.
J.D.K.
G.H.W.

Los Angeles, California
January, 1980

Table of Contents

Handbook of
APPELLATE ADVOCACY
Second Edition

*

Chapter One

STRUCTURE OF THE BRIEF

The advocate has some discretion over the writing style of the brief. However, the physical form of a brief is regulated by the rules of the appellate tribunal which has jurisdiction over the appeal. Among the elements of a brief regulated by these rules are the printing or typing format, size and weight of the paper, color of the manuscript cover, maximum length of the brief, and number of copies which must be submitted.

Remember that while a brief must be objective, it is also a persuasive document. Appearance, organization and content all serve to impress the court with the correctness of your position. Therefore, *every* section in the brief must be presented as professionally and as persuasively as possible.

The United States Supreme Court has propounded the Federal Rules of Appellate Procedure to govern the presentations of written briefs and appellate arguments in all federal appellate courts. These rules are contained in a published volume entitled Federal Rules of Appellate Procedure. In addition to the Federal Rules of Appellate Procedure, the Supreme Court and various courts of appeal have promulgated rules for their particular courts. These supplemental rules are published in separate volumes and in special portions of the reporters of these courts, such as in the "Court Rules" volume of the Supreme Court Digest.

Each state also has its own rules. In California, the most convenient source is the "Court Rules" volumes of the *West's Annotated California Codes* and the volume entitled "Rules" in *Deering's California Codes Annotated*. The local legal newspaper may also compile court rules, and publish them in the paper or in a loose-leaf publication.

I. TITLE PAGE

The purpose of the title page is to identify the appeal before the court, the parties to the case, and the party submitting the brief. This information is generally conveyed by a formalistic caption. The precise spacing and print required for this caption vary from court to court. Thus, the advocate must check the local rules. In the case of *Vitas v. Younger & Burton* an acceptable title page might look like this:

IN THE

SUPREME COURT OF THE UNITED STATES

OCTOBER TERM 1983

No. 81-8084

ROCKY VITAS,

                       Petitioner,

– AGAINST –

LORETTA YOUNGER and
MICHAEL BURTON,

                    Respondents.

ON WRIT OF CERTIORARI
TO THE UNITED STATES COURT OF APPEALS
FOR THE THIRTEENTH CIRCUIT

BRIEF FOR RESPONDENTS

Valerie B. Ackerman
Gina D. Liudzius

Counsel for Respondents
UCLA School of Law
405 Hilgard Avenue
Los Angeles, California 90024
(213) 825-1128

[D5895]

Note that the first statement identifies which court is hearing the
appeal. Next, the date of the term and the docket number of the

appeal are provided. Following this, the name of the case is given. Petitioner or appellant is always listed first in the United States Supreme Court and the respondent or appellee is listed second. The full names of the petitioner and respondent are given, as well as their procedural designation. Abbreviations of the party's name, such as "Younger, et al." are not used; generally "against" is used in lieu of "v."

After the name of the case, the title page explains the procedural posture of the case. If the case is an appeal, it is an appeal to the United States Supreme Court; but if the case is being heard on a writ of certiorari, writ is to the United States Court of Appeals for the applicable circuit. Below the procedural posture, the party submitting the brief is identified; and if the brief is a reply brief, that is indicated. All of this information is provided on the cover of the brief and on the first page of the text of the brief, just before the "Opinions Below."

One additional item of information is provided on the cover of the brief. On the lower right corner of the cover, the names, addresses, and phone numbers of counsel are indicated. Particular attention should be paid to punctuation, spacing, format, and print style.

II. QUESTIONS PRESENTED

The "Questions Presented" is the first persuasive section of the brief. The issues are couched as affirmative interrogatories so that an obvious and compelling answer is implied.

QUESTIONS PRESENTED

I. Whether a plaintiff whose stock purchase was a commercial transaction resulting in the sale of a business has stated a claim under the Securities Exchange Act of 1934.

II. Whether a plaintiff who fails to allege a nexus between the activities engaged in by the defendants and organized crime, has failed to allege that the defendants participated in conducting a RICO enterprise, and has failed to allege any racketeering enterprise injury has stated a claim under the Racketeer Influenced and Corrupt Organizations Act.

Note that the questions only describe the primary and determinative issues of the case. Subordinate points should, as much as possible, be incorporated in the questions concerning the main issue. Questions should be phrased to include significant facts relevant to the issue, but caution should be used to keep the question to a manageable length.

III. TOPICAL INDEX

The "Topical Index," like the table of contents of any book, is a complete listing of its various parts. It is a recapitulation of the sections, argument headings, and subheadings. Thus, it gives a thorough outline of the argument, enabling the reader to understand the argument and analysis.

TOPICAL INDEX

Note that all page numbers are typed "flush-right"; that is, the last digit of each page number is flush against the right-hand margin with everything backspaced from that point. The page number for each heading of the brief is lined up with the last line of text of that heading, and periods separated by spaces extend from the text up to two spaces before the last digit of each page number. The text of each heading is single spaced and indented in an outline form with a double space between each separate listing. All headings are typed in a style which matches the headings in the text. All other items listed in the topical index can be typed either in upper case letters, or in lower case letters with the initial letter of each word capitalized.

IV. TABLE OF AUTHORITIES

The "Table of Authorities" lists all the sources and references cited in the brief. This table is best categorized by groups with the categories arranged in the most persuasive order. Each category may in turn be subdivided into Supreme Court Cases, Appellate Cases, and District Court Cases.

All sources in the "Table of Authorities," like those in the body of the brief, must follow proper citation form. Both the official and unofficial citation for cases, as well as the subsequent history, should be included.

Note that the pages upon which each reference is cited are listed after the references. Here, as with the Topical Index, the page numbers are typed flush-right. When one case or statute is cited on numerous pages throughout the brief the advocate may use the designation *"passim"* in lieu of the page numbers. This designation should, however, be used sparingly.

V. OPINIONS BELOW

The opinions of the lower court from which the appeal is taken should be listed in "Opinions Below." This allows the reviewing court to become familiar with the previous opinion filed in the case. When the lower court's opinion is published, the citation for that opinion should be given. For example, in petitioner's brief for the appeal to the United States Supreme Court in *Textile Workers Union of America v. Darlington Manufacturing Company,* the Opinions Below section would state:

> The order of the National Labor Relations Board is found at 139 N.L.R.B. No. 23. The opinion of the United States Court of Appeals for the Fourth Circuit is found at 325 F.2d 682.

When the lower court's opinion has not been published, as in *Vitas v. Younger & Burton,* reference should be made to the relevant portion of the Transcript of Record.

OPINIONS BELOW

The opinion and order of the United States District Court for the District of Arcana is

unreported, and is contained in the Transcript of Record (R. 11-16). The opinion of
the United States Court of Appeals for the
Thirteenth Circuit is unreported, and is contained in the Transcript of Record (R. 17-22).

VI. JURISDICTIONAL STATEMENT

The United States Supreme Court and some courts of appeal
require petitioners and appellants to submit a "Statement of Jurisdiction." The respondent or appellee is not required to provide such a
statement, but one may optionally be included.

The "Statement of Jurisdiction" for a court of appeal outlines the
basis of jurisdiction for the federal district court, if the case originated
there, and the statutory basis for jurisdiction in the appellate court.
The "Statement of Jurisdiction" for United States Supreme Court briefs
should also refer to the statutory basis of jurisdiction and the facts
which qualify the case according to that statute.

When appealing to a state tribunal, the advocate should check the
local rules for the appropriate jurisdictional statement. In Moot Court
competition the jurisdictional statement is omitted. This does not
imply, however, that issues regarding jurisdiction which are raised by
the case are not discussed in the text.

VII. CONSTITUTIONAL PROVISIONS AND STATUTES INVOLVED

The United States Supreme Court Rules require a statement of the
constitutional provisions, treaties, statutes, ordinances, and regulations
involved in the case, or required for decision of the case. In addition,
the text of these applicable laws should be included in an appendix. In
Vitas v. Younger & Burton, respondents' brief would include the following statement:

STATUTES INVOLVED

The texts of the following statutes relevant to the determination of the present case
are set forth in appendices: Securities Exchange Act of 1934 § 3(a)(10), 15 U.S.C.
§ 78c(a)(10); Racketeer Influenced and Corrupt Organizations Act (''RICO''), 18 U.S.C.
§ 1961, <u>et seq</u>.

When statutes are known by the title of an act, both this title and
the various sections of the act, as well as the pertinent sections of the
code, should be given.

VIII. STATEMENT OF THE CASE

The most important of these preliminary statements is the exposition of the material facts in the "Statement of the Case." The statement must be objective; it must not state the facts erroneously or in a way which would create misleading or false inferences. In addition, only facts in the record should be cited and all material fact must be included, even though the fact may be damaging. Nevertheless, there is room for maneuvering; the impact which the facts have upon the court can be altered by changing the order in which they are presented, by emphasizing certain facts while merely mentioning others, and by skillfully choosing words and phrases.

Several other aspects of the statement also deserve attention. For every fact used the advocate should include a citation to the record from which the fact is taken. Furthermore, the statement should discuss the procedural history of the case. For example, the statement should indicate whether the suit is civil or criminal, what relief is sought, and what the lower court has decided.

In *Vitas v. Younger & Burton,* the Petitioner might state the facts as follows:

> Petitioner Rocky Vitas is a self-employed professional tennis player (R. 3). He purchased stock in Wholesale Computer, Inc. (''WCI''), from Respondents Loretta Younger and Michael Burton, both former directors, officers and shareholders of the company (R. 3).
>
> Mr. Vitas first met Younger on November 1, 1982, at which time she proposed that he buy her 100 shares of WCI stock. She represented that the corporation had operated profitably each year after 1977, that its profit for 1981 was in excess of $150,000, and that its prospects were very good. She further stated that Burton was completely responsible for all operations of the company, which depended upon his personal contacts for its success. Mr. Vitas would have no duties whatsoever with respect to WCI (R. 4). Younger explained that she wished to sell her shares in order to purchase an interest in a company that owned orange groves in Florida (R. 4).
>
> In reliance upon Younger's representations, Mr. Vitas agreed to buy all her shares

for $500,000, provided that he could also purchase at least 50 other shares. (Mr. Vitas had a total of $800,000 saved which he wished to invest.) Younger said that Burton would sell his 50 shares, provided Mr. Vitas continued Burton's long-term employment contract with the company. Mr. Vitas agreed. He pledged $150,000 for Burton's shares (R. 4).

On November 8, 1982, Mr. Vitas met with James Madison, the holder of the 50 remaining shares in WCI. Madison showed Mr. Vitas a letter which Younger had written stating: ''All you'll have to do is sit back and let Mike Burton make your money work'' (R. 5).

The purchase agreement contained warranties from Younger and Burton that they were unaware of any adverse developments concerning WCI occurring after June 30, 1982 (R. 6). At the closing, on November 22, Burton became Chair and President of the company, and, at his request, his annual bonus was increased to one-half of the company's after-tax profit (R. 6). Mr. Vitas took no active role in the management of the company (R. 6).

February 21, 1983, Mr. Vitas received the audited 1982 financial statements showing a loss in excess of $50,000 for the year (R. 6). He questioned Burton the next day, and Burton admitted that he had been seriously ill since July 1982. This had drastically curtailed his effectiveness, and was directly responsible for the company's financial loss. Burton had confided in Younger about his illness the previous August, and she advised him to say nothing. She told him she would bail them out (R. 7). Subsequently, Younger developed the fraudulent scheme which enabled them to sell their stock and invest together in Florida Oranges, Inc. (R. 7).

Mr. Vitas brought suit against Burton and Younger in the District Court of Arcana. The first cause of action, alleging violations of Section 10(b) of the Securities Exchange Act of 1934 and Rule 10b-5 promulgated thereunder, survived a motion to dismiss. The sec-

ond, predicated upon a violation of the Racketeer Influenced and Corrupt Organizations
Act of 1970 (''RICO'') was dismissed pursuant
to Fed.R.Cir.P. 12(b)(6). On interlocutory
appeal, the United States Court of Appeals for
the Thirteenth Circuit dismissed both causes
of action. Petitioner subsequently petitioned this Court for a writ of certiorari, which
was granted on July 18, 1983.

The Respondent, on the other hand, could state the same set of facts in
another way:

Respondents Loretta Younger (''Younger'')
and Michael Burton (''Burton'') are the former owners of Wholesale Computer, Inc.
(''Wholesale Computer''), a computer equip-
ment supplier which operated profitably from
1977 through August, 1982. Younger served as
President and Chairman of the Board and the
owner of 50% of the business, while Burton was
the Vice President and a 25% owner (R. 3).
James Madison (''Madison'') also held an interest in the corporation, but took no part in
the operation of the business (R. 5). In
July, 1982, Burton became seriously ill and
unable to fully perform his duties. Upon
hearing of Burton's illness in August, Younger promised to sell the business (R. 7).

In October, 1982, Petitioner Rocky Vitas
(''Vitas''), a former professional tennis
player, became interested in acquiring a
business property with $800,000 he had saved
from tournament winnings (R. 3-4). Vitas'
cousin and close friend, Able Savant (''Savant''), an important Wholesale Computer customer, encouraged Vitas to meet with Younger
to discuss the acquisition of that business
(R. 4).

On November 1, 1982, Vitas and Savant met
with Younger to discuss the purchase of Younger's shares in Wholesale Computer (R. 4).
Vitas agreed to buy Younger's 50% share of the
business, upon the express condition that he
could also acquire at least another 25% of the
business, which would effectively give him

complete control over Wholesale Computer (R. 4-5).

In a meeting on November 8, 1982, Madison showed Vitas a letter, purportedly written by Younger, which stated that Wholesale Computer's prospects were favorable (R. 5). Savant's accountant scrutinized Wholesale Computer's books and verified the company's potential for continued profitability through June 30, 1982 (R. 6).

By November 22, 1982, Vitas had paid a total of $650,000 for his controlling 75% interest in the business. As the new owner, Vitas asked Burton to assume Younger's duties in addition to his usual obligations, and altered Burton's contract to include an annual bonus of one-half the company's after tax profit (R. 6). Burton and Younger invested the proceeds of the sale in a different business opportunity, Florida Oranges, Inc. (R. 7).

Unfortunately, upon receiving Wholesale Computer's 1982 audited financial statements, Vitas discovered that the business had suffered a $50,000 loss in the latter half of 1982. When Vitas confronted Burton with this information, Burton revealed that he had been seriously ill since July, 1982, and had been unable to capitalize on his personal contacts in the computer business (R. 7). Without giving Burton an opportunity to bring Wholesale Computer out of its financial slump, Vitas demanded Burton's resignation (R. 7) and filed this action in the United States District Court, District of Arcana. Vitas alleged that in connection with selling the business, Burton and Younger had violated Section 10(b) of the Securities Exchange Act of 1934 (''1934 Act'') and Rule 10b-5 promulgated thereunder, and the Racketeer Influenced and Corrupt Organizations Act (''RICO''), 18 U.S.C. § 1962(c). Vitas not only seeks $650,000 in damages on his securities claim, but an additional $1.3 million and attorney's fees under RICO's civil damages provisions (R. 10), 18 U.S.C. § 1964(c).

Respondents moved to dismiss the claim under Federal Rules of Civil Procedure 12(b)(1)
and 12(b)(6) for lack of subject matter jurisdiction and failure to state a claim. The
district court denied the motion to dismiss
the securities claim, but dismissed the RICO
claim, finding it deficient for failing to allege either the existence of an ''enterprise'' or a ''racketeering enterprise injury'' (R. 15).

On interlocutory appeal, the Thirteenth
Circuit Court of Appeals reversed the district court's ruling on the securities claim.
The court held that the sale of Wholesale Computer was a sale of a business and not within
the reach of the 1934 Act. In addition, the
court affirmed the dismissal of the RICO
claim, noting that Congress never intended
RICO to extend to ''garden variety'' securities cases (R. 20-21).

On July 18, 1983, this Court granted <u>certi-
orari</u> to consider the questions raised by the
record.

IX. SUMMARY OF ARGUMENT

The "Summary of Argument" is a terse statement of the advocate's
main contentions in the same order as they appear in the brief. It
contains only those propositions which are crucial to the case, with
each argument set forth in separate paragraphs. Minor points should
not be presented. Likewise, it is not necessary to cite legal authorities,
unless a particular argument rests primarily upon an examination of
those authorities.

If a judge has not read the entire brief prior to oral argument, the
Summary of Argument is a valuable substitute which the judge can
peruse quickly prior to the hearing. Therefore, many advocates firmly
believe that the Summary of Argument is one of the most important
sections of the brief, recapitulating the central issues in the case. The
Summary of Argument for Respondents in *Vitas v. Younger & Burton*
appears as follows:

Although ''stock'' expressly appears in
the statutory definition of a security, the
Supreme Court has rejected a literal interpretation of the definition when stock transactions result in the sale of a business.

This substance-over-form approach looks to the ''economic realities'' of the underlying transaction. The statutory definition itself requires a transactional analysis because it contains the prefatory clause ''unless the context otherwise requires.'' Moreover, the sale of business exception is consistent with congressional intent to exclude private, commercial transactions from the scope of securities legislation and to reserve the protections of these laws for passive investors rather than entrepreneurs.

In the present case, Vitas has failed to state a proper claim under the 1934 Act because his 75% stock purchase was in ''economic reality'' a commercial transaction effecting the sale of a business. By virtue of his 75% majority ownership of Wholesale Computer, Vitas was in a position to control the success of his investment, quite unlike the passive investor who relinquishes control to a third party. By making critical decisions concerning the management of Wholesale Computer, Vitas demonstrated that he was not ''relying'' on others within the meaning of a securities investment.

Because Vitas' stock purchase did not involve a ''security'' within the meaning of the 1934 Act, the Court of Appeals correctly dismissed his securities claims and its decision should be affirmed.

Vitas has also failed to state a claim under the Racketeer Influenced and Corrupt Organizations Act (''RICO''). The alleged ''racketeering activities,'' misrepresentations in the sale of a small business, are hardly the sort of ''organized crime'' which prompted a ''full scale attack'' by Congress when it enacted RICO. Although Congress made ''fraud in the sale of securities'' a RICO predicate act, the legislative history of the provision discloses that the activities of Burton and Younger do not constitute ''organized crime'' in any sense of the word.

```
     Moreover, Vitas has failed to allege that
Burton and Younger participated in the con-
trol of any entity that can reasonably be
termed a RICO enterprise.  Vitas alleges no
more than a pattern of racketeering activity
on the part of Burton and Younger.

     Finally, Vitas seeks treble damages based
on his allegation that he has been injured by
racketeering activities.  Compelling policy
concerns justify this Court's denial of RICO
standing to Vitas, who has not alleged ''rack-
eteering enterprise injury.''  Construed in
the light most favorable to Vitas, his Com-
plaint fails to allege injury of the sort Con-
gress sought to remedy by enacting RICO.
Vitas should be denied access to a federal fo-
rum and to the overly harsh penalty of treble
damages because he has suffered nothing more
than injury by reason of misrepresentations,
for which he enjoys adequate remedies in state
court.
```

X. ARGUMENT

The "Argument" is the body of the brief where the contentions, legal analysis, and supporting authority are set forth. Since the various methods of writing persuasive arguments are discussed at length in Chapter Two, this section is devoted to the structuring of headings and captions.

The purpose of headings is to explain, in a persuasive manner, the facts and analysis which follow. As a result, the headings should refer to specific facts of the case, and should be argumentative in tone. To convey effectively the intended message, captions should not exceed five lines in length.

The main contention is numbered with roman numerals centered above the text of the contention. The contention itself is typed in capitals, and positioned with margins of equal size. The lines of the caption should be as close in length as possible; and whole phrases should be kept, to the extent possible, on the same line. If the caption cannot be typed as a perfect block, the text following the first line of the contention should be typed in lines of successively decreasing length. Each line, however, should have margins of roughly equal length:

II.

VITAS HAS FAILED TO STATE A CLAIM COGNIZABLE
UNDER THE RACKETEER INFLUENCED AND CORRUPT
ORGANIZATIONS ACT

The contentions, as well as all other captions within the Argument, should be in the form of complete sentences.

The headings are also typed in capitals and are designated alphabetically with capital letters. The first line of the heading is positioned with the capital letter placed five spaces in from the margin, followed by a period and two spaces. The text of the heading is typed in block form with each succeeding line of the heading beginning and ending under the preceding line:

A. VITAS HAS FAILED TO ALLEGE THAT BURTON AND
   YOUNGER PARTICIPATED IN ORGANIZED CRIMINAL
   ACTIVITY COGNIZABLE UNDER RICO

Headings within a contention should be used only when two or more headings follow the contention; when only one exists, the advocate should eliminate the heading and place the uninterrupted text under the contention. The advocate should be careful always to separate contentions, headings, and subheadings with textual information. A heading should never directly follow a contention.

The subheadings are typed in lower case letters, and the entire subheading should be underlined. Consecutive arabic numerals are used to designate each subheading within a heading. The first line of the subheading is positioned with the arabic numeral placed ten spaces in from the margin followed by a period and two spaces. Like the heading, the subheading is typed as a column, with each succeeding line beginning under the first word in the first line of the subheading:

2. The activities of Burton and Younger do not
   constitute ''organized crime'' cognizable
   under RICO

Subheadings are not used unless two or more follow the heading. If only one subheading exists it should be eliminated and the text of the argument should be typed without interruption. Textual information always separates a subheading from another subheading or the preceding heading.

Generally speaking, the advocate should limit subdivision of arguments to three levels of analysis—contentions, headings, and subheadings. Further subdivision tends to decrease persuasiveness of the captions as a whole and may cause confusion to the court reading the brief.

XI.   CONCLUSION

The "Conclusion" is little more than a restatement of the relief prayed. The advocate should not hesitate to ask for alternative remedies, where appropriate. In particularly lengthy or complex briefs, the conclusion may also recapitulate the primary arguments which justify the relief sought:

```
                      CONCLUSION
     For the reasons set forth above, Respon-
dents respectfully request that the judgment
of the United States Court of Appeals for the
Thirteenth Circuit be affirmed, and that
Vitas' claims be dismissed for lack of subject
matter jurisdiction and failure to state a
claim.

                       Respectfully submit-
                       ted,


                       _____

                       Valerie B. Ackerman


                       _____

                       Gina D. Liudzius
                       Attorneys for
                       Respondents
```

Note that the attorneys sign the brief above their typed names. It is not required that all attorneys who have helped to draft the brief sign it. One signature line containing the signature of the senior attorney can be placed above a list of the typed names of the other attorneys who participated in the drafting of the brief.

XII.   APPENDICES

"Appendices" to written briefs are analogous to exhibits attached to trial court pleadings—they refer the court to vitally relevant information which must be set out verbatim. Appendices to written briefs usually are composed of the constitutional provisions, statutes, and regulations which are the legal foundations for the contentions in the brief. The complete text of the legislative enactments need not be reproduced; the advocate may, for the sake of brevity, provide only those parts of the enactments which relate to the contentions. When excerpting portions of statutes and constitutional provisions, however, the advocate must indicate explicitly that the enactment is not set out in full:

APPENDIX A

Securities Act of 1933:

    15 U.S.C. § 77b(1) (1982):

    2. When used in this title, unless the context otherwise requires:

        (1) The term ''security'' means any note, stock, treasury stock, bond, debenture, evidence of indebtedness, certificate of interest or participation in any profit-sharing agreement.

Securities Exchange Act of 1934:

    15 U.S.C. § 78c(a)(10) (1982):

    3. (a) When used in this title, unless the context otherwise requires:

        . . . .

        (10) The term ''security'' means any note, stock, treasury stock, bond, debenture, certificate of interest or participation in any profit-sharing agreement, or in any oil, gas, or other mineral royalty or lease, any collateral-trust certificate, preorganization certificate or subscription, transferable share, investment contract, voting-trust certificate, certificate of deposit, for a security, or in general, any instrument commonly known as a ''security''; or any certificate of interest or participation in, temporary or interim certificate for, receipt for, or warrant or right to subscribe to or purchase, any of the foregoing; but shall not include currency or any note, draft, bill of exchange, or banker's acceptance which has a maturity at the time of issuance of not exceeding nine months, exclusive of days of grace, or any renewal thereof the maturity of which is likewise limited.

In addition to constitutional provisions and legislative enactments, the advocate may also use appendices to provide the court with statistics, graphs, or other information pertinent to the case. Each item should be placed in a separate appendix, and the appendices should be designated by consecutive capital letters.

Chapter Two

PERSUASIVE BRIEF WRITING

Mastering the art of persuasive brief writing requires both time and effort. To be successful, an appellate advocate must select and arrange arguments effectively. Use various methods of structuring sentences and paragraphs, and use persuasive words to enhance legal propositions. Analyze precedents and statutes to support contentions and to distinguish unfavorable legal authorities. These elements of persuasive brief writing will enable the court to understand the facts and legal contentions advanced, and will persuade the court of the correct legal and equitable determination of the case.

The written brief constitutes the principal argument of the case. The brief is not a scholarly, objective discourse on a specific area of the law. An advocate must be fair and accurate, but the brief must be a forceful and eloquent argument that justice is best served by a particular legal result.

The brief is crucial to an appeal. In jurisdictions where oral arguments have been restricted or eliminated, the brief serves as the primary, and perhaps only, persuasive tool for presenting a particular client's case. Moreover, even when oral arguments are not restricted, the brief is generally the strongest and most effective way to convey a legal argument to the court. Although legal writing requires a particular technical style, all good writing should be clear, concise, accurate, and persuasive.

I. PREPARING TO WRITE THE BRIEF

Before drafting the brief, a number of preliminary steps must first be completed. These include gaining a thorough knowledge of the facts and procedural posture of the case, extensively researching applicable law, and becoming familiar with the court which will decide the appeal. In practice these steps overlap. Thus, when concentrating on learning the case, an advocate should also begin developing potential arguments, theories, and examples. Likewise, review the facts of the case, if necessary, while researching.

A. KNOW THE CASE

The first step in preparing an appellate brief is to become completely familiar with the case. The facts and the record will determine the areas of the law to research and will provide the issues and the potential for reversible errors. Additionally, credibility with the court will depend upon your command of the facts and of the record.

1. Facts of the Case

Every fact in the case should be known, including the parties, their relationship to each other, and the actions each party has taken. In some cases it might be helpful at the outset to make a chronology of events. This is also a good opportunity to write an initial statement of facts.

At this initial stage it may not be possible to tell which facts are most important and which facts you will wish to emphasize. Therefore, expect to edit the preliminary statement of facts before including it in the brief.

2. Record and Procedural Posture of the Case

Read the entire record carefully. A thoroughly prepared advocate should be able to recall the page in the record on which particular information can be found. This "geographical familiarity" with the record aids brief writing and argument. What is the procedural posture of the case? What is the holding of the court below and the basis for its decision? What were the findings of fact and law? For example, in the *Vitas* case, the motion to dismiss was based upon Federal Rules of Civil Procedure 12(b)(1) and 12(b)(6). One of Vitas's two claims for relief was dismissed by the district court. On appeal, both claims were dismissed by the court of appeal. Vitas, as petitioner, then sought a reversal of the court of appeal's decision.

In the thick of the issues and the research it is easy to lose track of the procedural posture of the case, and of the different burdens carried by parties seeking to uphold or to reverse a lower court's decision.

Thus, many beginning advocates spend needless energy attempting to prove what is already presumed in their favor. Furthermore, an advocate must be forceful, but must also set forth allegations of error in a manner reflecting professional competence and respect for the court. The court is unlikely to read a brief sympathetically if it seems disrespectful to the lower court or includes personal attacks on the court or opposing counsel.

An effective appellant's brief must convince the court that the lower court's decision resulted in some major injustice against the client. This attitude must translate itself both into the tone and substance of the brief, with appellant's counsel capturing that attitude of redressing an injustice with forceful legal and policy arguments based on the facts of the case.

In contrast, the respondent's brief must reassure the court that no injustice has been done by the lower court. An error must be shown to be harmless. The attitude which counsel for respondent should portray must fit this purpose. Respondent's brief should, in tone and substance, be structured within a calm and rational approach which explains not only the reasonableness of the lower court action, but also emphasizes the fact that any errors which might have occurred did not cause the appellant any injustice.

3. Standard of Review

Before factual and legal arguments can be marshalled effectively, the precise standard of review governing the case must be determined, and the factual and legal arguments must be cast in a manner which will satisfy that standard. An advocate must prove, for example, that the lower court was clearly wrong, or that the lower court abused its discretion, or that there is no set of facts which would entitle the other party to relief. Appellate judges routinely ask advocates to identify the standard of review at oral argument. In some jurisdictions, a statement concerning the standard of review in the brief is required. Regardless, if a brief does not address the standard of review, a void is left which will be filled by opposing counsel, or the judges, or the judges' clerks.

4. Theory of the Case

Before writing the brief, an advocate must have a clear idea of what the client's case is about and why the court should rule in the client's favor. The record will limit theories of the case to some degree. Nevertheless, new theories may be presented or earlier theories may be presented in a new light. While learning the case, keep the following points in mind:

(1) Isolate the critical areas of the case;

(2) Determine the relative importance of legal and factual issues;

(3) Assess the record and the legal authorities objectively to see where they support or do not support the issues on both sides;

(4) Construct a persuasive argument and clearly convey that argument to the court.

B. RESEARCH

While a complete discussion of conducting legal research is beyond the scope of this book, it is important to emphasize some major points.

1. General Guidelines

The facts of the case and the record will define the initial issues to be researched. As the research progresses, which issues to emphasize and which to disregard should be apparent. Selection of issues will be discussed in the next section. Keep in mind that thorough research will include the sociological and economic implications of the case as well as legal principles. The advocate should also be ready to discuss the interests of the community in the outcome of this case.

Extensive research enables the advocate to determine the issues involved in the appeal, guides the advocate in developing strategy and supporting arguments, and indicates the relative strengths and weaknesses of his or her contentions. The research also assists in anticipating arguments which will be raised and facts which will be emphasized by opposing counsel. Finally, thorough research will provide a sense of the trend of the courts in a particular area of the law.

Remember to explore not only case law, but also applicable statutes and regulations, and their subsequent amendments and judicial interpretations. Shepardize *all* precedents and statutes intended to be relied upon. There is no greater embarrassment to the advocate, nor greater disservice to the client, than to rely on overruled precedents or repealed legislative enactments.

An understanding of how a particular court views different procedural issues and treats particular types of reversible error may be invaluable in determining which issues to present to the court, and how these issues can be successfully argued. This is particularly true of state or federal supreme courts, and appellate courts in which the advocate knows which judges will be hearing the appeal.

While doing your research, keep in mind the policy issues the court may face in this case and how the court has addressed similar policy considerations in previous cases. Policy considerations will be especially important where the court is interpreting a statute for the first time or where the court may reverse or limit former decisional rules. If possible, read the appellate briefs of cases relied upon. This research may lead to a deeper understanding of the court's present position and the rationales behind that stance, as well as additional policy arguments.

2. Organization of Research

It is useful from the very outset to organize material as it is gathered. Several methods are suggested by way of illustration. A card index may be kept of the cases and material read. An outline or digest may be organized by issues. Comparing the holdings of the various circuits or states, information may be put into a matrix to provide a quick reference later. Although this organization may seem time consuming, the initial effort will save time spent searching through notes and will also help prepare for oral argument.

CHECKLIST

PRIOR TO WRITING

(Items to make sure research is essentially complete and to keep in mind when drafting the brief.)

I. *Know the Case*

  1. What are the facts of the case?

  2. What is the procedural posture of the case?

  3. What is the judgment or order of the lower court?

  4. On what basis did the lower court make its decision (i.e.—what are the findings of fact and law)?

  5. What is the burden of proof on appeal and on the parties?

  6. What standard must the appellate court apply to uphold or reverse the lower court's decision?

  7. What state and federal statutes, codes, and constitutional provisions are applicable?

  8. Specify the exact relief you seek from the appellate court.

II. *Is research complete?*

  1. Have you identified the issues?

  2. Have you identified the controlling cases?

  3. Have all cases and statutes been Shepardized?

  4. What is the fact situation of each of the controlling cases?

  5. How is each main case distinguished from, or similar to, other cases?

  6. What is the holding and what is the dictum of each case?

  7. Have you identified conflicts between circuits or between states?

  8. Have you researched code and statute annotations?

  9. Have you researched applicable legislative history?

  10. Are you familiar with the court rules of the appellate court?

II. SELECTING AND ARRANGING THE CONTENTIONS TO BE PRESENTED

After studying the facts in the record and extensively researching applicable areas of law which apply to these facts, the contentions to be argued must be selected and arranged in the brief. Depending upon the facts of the case and what has been gleaned from research, a

particular statutory construction, repudiation of a prior judicial principle, or enunciation of a new doctrine by the reviewing court may be
argued. The strategy chosen will determine the most persuasive issues
to be argued and the most effective order in which they can be
presented to the court.

A. SELECTION OF THE ISSUES

Every case will involve a multitude of legal issues. It is an
advocate's task to select only those issues which will persuade the
court. For the purposes of persuasion and clarity, the brief should
address only the primary issues.

First determine whether, as a technical matter, the issue can be
raised at all. If the issue was not raised in the trial court, the appellate
court may not have jurisdiction to even consider the issue. After
determining which issues can be raised on appeal, legal authorities,
case facts, and other supporting material must be found which bear
upon each issue. With this information consider the effect of arguing
each issue, how the issue will affect the client's case, and the ramifications that a successful determination would have on future cases
involving the same issue.

Analyze each issue individually, then assess the relative value of
each. Some issues will be both legally supportable and crucial to a
successful determination of the case. Others will be relevant to the
facts of the case, but will most likely be decided against the client. Still
others, while legally supportable, will not aid in winning the case.
Obviously, those issues which are both central to the case and strongly
supported by case law will be retained and included in the brief. The
difficulty occurs in deciding the fate of those issues which are weak, or
seemingly inconsequential or tangential.

A relevant but legally unsupportable issue should either be conceded or discussed briefly. An irrelevant issue should not be used. It is
likely to detract from or even be fatal to the entire case by obscuring
the main issues and distracting the court's attention from the strengths
of the case. Legally supportable, but seemingly weak, inconsequential
and tangential issues should not be dismissed summarily. Such issues
might be combined with other issues which have stronger support.
Inevitably, some issues must be abandoned. Remember, the goal is to
achieve a certain judgment, not to discuss every issue touched upon by
the facts of the case.

B. ARTICULATING THE ISSUES AS CONTENTIONS

After selection, the issues must be phrased to state contentions. A
contention, or point heading, is an assertive and positive statement of
an issue which clearly indicates how the advocate believes the issue
should be resolved. Contentions should embody the issue under consid-

eration and explicitly provide the determination you want the court to reach. Contentions explicitly refer to parties and facts involved in the particular appeal and should be articulated in short, direct sentences with verbs in the active voice. Thus, issues from the petitioner's brief in the Vitas case would be stated as contentions in the following manner:

Issue:

Whether the court should read an organized crime requirement into RICO.

Contention:

An organized crime requirement would subvert Congressional intent and raise serious constitutional difficulties.

Issue:

Whether Congress intended to protect investors like Mr. Vitas under the Securities Exchange Act.

Contention:

Mr. Vitas is an investor deserving the protection of the 1934 Act, not an entrepreneur intending to manage a business.

Respondent would state the same issues as contentions in the following manner:

Issue:

Whether the court should read an organized crime requirement into RICO.

Contention:

RICO is intended to provide sanctions and remedies against those engaged in activity characteristic of organized crime.

Issue:

Whether Congress intended to protect investors like Mr. Vitas under the Securities Exchange Act.

Contention:

Because Vitas' stock purchase resulted in the sale of a business, the federal securities laws are inapplicable.

C. ARRANGEMENT OF THE CONTENTIONS IN THE BRIEF

Once the issues are selected and stated as contentions, arrange them in a persuasive and logical order. Each contention should be arranged to build upon the preceding one within the structure of the chosen strategy. The conclusion should logically follow from the propositions established in the contentions. Start with a strong contention. If the case depends upon a "threshold issue," the "threshold issue" should be used as the lead contention. For example, if the respondent can convince the court in the Vitas case, that a RICO claim requires an allegation of organized crime, then the court can quickly decide that aspect of the case without discussing other elements of a RICO claim. This contention might be stated as follows:

```
Mr. Vitas fails to state a claim under RICO
because he fails to allege any tie to organ-
ized crime.
```

After choosing a persuasive lead contention, arrange the contentions in a logical and effective manner. One approach is to present the contentions so as to complement the chronology of the case. This method is most effective when various legal issues arise out of actions which occurred at different times prior to the commencement of litigation. Another method is to arrange the contentions through the deductive or inductive methods of reasoning. The deductive method proceeds from very general and readily acceptable contentions to those which are very specific and which require a greater amount of persuasion. The inductive method, in contrast, proves narrow, specific contentions first, and then builds upon these, concluding with a general, summary contention. The effectiveness of each method varies, depending upon the facts of the case and the legal issues to be argued.

Two divergent points of view exist as to the effectiveness of strong concluding contentions. Some appellate attorneys believe that an argument should conclude with a relatively strong contention, as judges often remember best what was read last.

Other attorneys believe that a judge, reading through a lengthy brief, will naturally tire and lose interest and may miss important issues if not presented early in the brief. Moreover, a judge, having determined that the first contentions are without merit, may unconsciously decide the final issues similarly. Therefore the strongest and most persuasive contentions appear first, and the weaker contentions should be placed at the end of the brief.

Regardless of which format is chosen, the argument, in its entirety, should proceed logically and persuasively as the judge reads through the arrangement of the contentions. The first breakdown of a contention should divide it into a small number of headings which must be demonstrated if the contention is to be proven. Each heading should deal with only one facet of the contention. Headings thus serve as mini-contentions which, when proven, establish the validity of the main contention.

In this sense, headings bear the same relationship to the contention as elements of a cause of action bear to the cause of action itself. The cause of action for fraud, for example, consists of the elements of representation, falsity of the representation, knowledge or intent, reliance by the victim, and resulting damage to the victim. Assume that Betty sold her car to Bob for $1,000, claiming that she had just installed a new transmission in the car. After Bob drove the newly purchased car for a few hours, the transmission proved defective; the mechanic who charged Bob $400 to repair the transmission told him that the purportedly new transmission was actually five years old. If Bob were to argue at the appellate level that he should recover damages due to the fraudulent misrepresentation by Betty regarding the age of the transmission, his contention and headings might look something like this:

I. FRAUDULENT MISREPRESENTATION OF THE AGE OF THE TRANSMISSION CAUSED BOB DAMAGES IN THE AMOUNT OF FOUR HUNDRED DOLLARS.

   A. BETTY REPRESENTED TO BOB THAT THE TRANSMISSION IN THE CAR WAS NEW AT THE TIME THAT BOB PURCHASED THE CAR FROM HER.

   B. BETTY'S REPRESENTATION THAT THE CAR CONTAINED A NEW TRANSMISSION WAS FALSE.

   C. AT THE TIME THAT BETTY REPRESENTED TO BOB THAT THE TRANSMISSION WAS NEW, BETTY KNEW THAT THIS REPRESENTATION WAS FALSE.

   D. BOB RELIED UPON BETTY'S REPRESENTATION THAT THE TRANSMISSION WAS NEW WHEN PURCHASING BETTY'S CAR.

   E. AS A RESULT OF BOB'S RELIANCE ON BETTY'S MISREPRESENTATION AS TO THE AGE OF THE TRANSMISSION, BOB WAS DAMAGED IN THE AMOUNT OF FOUR HUNDRED DOLLARS.

In this example, each of the headings must be proved if Bob is to be successful on appeal. The contention that Betty acted fraudulently can be proved only by Bob establishing that the headings, which comprise the elements of fraud, are true. If any of these headings is disproved, the contention itself fails. Thus, the headings are those subissues which must be proved if the contention is to succeed.

Counsel for Petitioner in *Vitas v. Younger & Burton* argued that the court of appeals erred in dismissing petitioner's securities claim on the basis that his stock purchase was not a "securities transaction" within the meaning of the Securities Exchange Act of 1934. In earlier securities cases, the United States Supreme Court enunciated a test for determining when sale of stock is a securities transaction. Petitioner contended that this test is not applicable in the particular factual setting of the case, and that even if the test were to be applied, a securities transaction did take place. Given these legal and factual issues which must be proven if the dismissal is to be reversed, counsel for petitioner in *Vitas* outlined her contention and supporting headings as follows:

I. THE COURT OF APPEALS ERRED IN ORDERING DIS-
MISSAL OF MR. VITAS' SECURITIES CLAIM FOR
LACK OF SUBJECT MATTER JURISDICTION BE-
CAUSE THE STOCK SALE WAS A ''SECURITIES
TRANSACTION'' REGULATED BY THE 1934 ACT

   A. THE <u>HOWEY-FORMAN</u> ECONOMIC REALITIES
      TEST DOES NOT APPLY TO THIS SALE OF OR-
      DINARY CORPORATE STOCK

   B. EVEN ASSUMING THAT THE <u>HOWEY-FORMAN</u>
      TEST APPLIES IN THIS CASE, THERE IS A
      ''SECURITIES TRANSACTION'' WITHIN THE
      MEANING OF THE 1934 ACT

So arranged, the contention and its supporting headings provide a skeletal outline of the argument of the contention.

After selecting and arranging the headings necessary to prove the contention, each heading must be divided into subheadings. Subheadings are the detailed elements which must be demonstrated if the heading is to be proven. A detailed version of the contention relating to the dismissal in *Vitas* might be constructed as follows:

I. THE COURT OF APPEALS ERRED IN ORDERING DIS-
MISSAL OF MR. VITAS' SECURITIES CLAIM FOR
LACK OF SUBJECT MATTER JURISDICTION BE-
CAUSE THE STOCK SALE WAS A ''SECURITIES
TRANSACTION'' REGULATED BY THE 1934 ACT

   A. THE <u>HOWEY-FORMAN</u> ECONOMIC REALITIES
      TEST DOES NOT APPLY TO THIS SALE OF OR-
      DINARY CORPORATE STOCK

      1. <u>Forman</u> suggests two separate and dis-
         tinct economic realities tests for
         determining whether federal securi-

ties law applies; Mr. Vitas satisfies the first test

2. This Court's decisions since Forman
support protecting purchasers of ordinary corporate stock

3. Important policy and administrative
concerns emphasize the need for federal securities law protection of defrauded buyers of ordinary corporate
stock

B. EVEN ASSUMING THAT THE HOWEY–FORMAN
TEST APPLIES IN THIS CASE, THERE IS A
''SECURITIES TRANSACTION'' WITHIN THE
MEANING OF THE 1934 ACT

1. Mr. Vitas satisfies the Howey–Forman
test because he purchased the stock
while relying solely on Burton's managerial efforts

2. Mr. Vitas is an investor deserving
the protection of the 1934 Act, not
an entrepreneur intending to manage a
business

This outline demonstrates that each element of the contention is a step
in the reasoning process validating the contention. The headings
provide proof of the contention, and additionally serve as the topic or
theme, for each segment of the argument.

So structured, the contention with its headings and subheadings
provides the court with a logical and persuasive argument for deciding
the issue in your favor. To increase the persuasive quality, begin the
discussion of each contention with an introductory paragraph setting
forth a summary of the contention culled from the headings and
subheadings. After arguing the headings and the subheadings, conclude the discussion of the contention with a final paragraph summarizing the argument and demonstrating that the proof of the contention is
inevitable from the proof of the headings and subheadings.

III. PERSUASIVE WRITING TECHNIQUES

A. GENERAL GUIDELINES

An effective advocate not only develops sound legal propositions,
but also presents those propositions persuasively. The key principles of
persuasive writing are clarity, brevity, and accuracy.

Communicate in simple, understandable terms. The court can be
persuaded only if it can comprehend the arguments and reasoning

presented. In order to be understood, avoid turgid writing and torturous reasoning. This is not an easy task. Most legal issues are by their nature complex and the language of the law abounds with highly technical terms which, when strung together, may be unintelligible to all but the most skilled legal mind. Clarity can be achieved only through a continual process of drafting and redrafting the brief with the intent of communicating the argument in the simplest, clearest terms possible.

The quality of a brief is not related to its length. Courts are persuaded not by the sheer mass of material presented, but by the selective use and analysis of the relevant law. Brevity enhances clarity, and clear arguments are what persuade judges.

Briefs must, of course, be accurate. Misstatements will erode the court's confidence in the writer. If the court feels that the brief does not present a fair and accurate version of the facts and law, the court will not be persuaded by the arguments in the brief. To insure accuracy, verify that all quotations and citations are correct and used in the proper context. You must also insure that the presentation of all of the facts is accurate.

B. EDITING

Revising is a necessary part of persuasive writing. Few writers are capable of producing exactly what they want on the first try.

Indeed, few writers would even think of publishing an unedited law review article or book, yet some lawyers seem surprisingly casual about filing unedited briefs with the court. Some of the following techniques may help your editing process:

1. Have a colleague read and critique your brief.

2. Read your brief out loud. If the material cannot be spoken with ease, it should be rewritten.

3. If possible, allow a gap of a day or two between drafts. This allows you to gain a fresh perspective.

4. On reading your own work, ask yourself:

    a. Does it say what I mean to say?

    b. Does each sentence, paragraph, or word help to make the point?

    c. Is each sentence, paragraph, or word necessary?

    d. Is it *really* necessary?

Editing is a painful process. All writers become attached to their ideas and may be unwilling to sacrifice portions of their masterpiece. But all writing improves with editing. This important phase of brief writing must not be overlooked.

C. STRUCTURE AND USE OF SENTENCES

No established formula exists for using words and sentences; they must be individually tailored to fit the needs and requirements of the topic being argued and your particular writing style. Some general guidelines are possible.

Whenever possible, use the active voice to present ideas in a more forceful, concise manner. Obviously, however, the passive voice should be used when it helps to make a point more effectively.

Sentences should be linked to the topic sentence to provide continuity and flow within the paragraph. The use of transitional words can be effectively used to bridge sentences:

accordingly	furthermore	likewise
although	hence	moreover
as a result		
but	however	nevertheless
consequently	in addition	similarly
for example	incidentally	such

Avoid very long sentences or many very short sentences. The goal of sentence structure is to pace the court in its reading of the argument with long, short, and medium length sentences. The desired blend depends upon the message or mood you wish to convey. A short sentence, for example, is an effective means of emphasizing an important thought, especially if it appears at the end of a string of longer sentences, or at the conclusion of a lengthy paragraph. The lack of descriptive words makes the sentence stand out, stating clearly and concisely the intended idea. A series of short sentences may imply a cold and hostile emotion, while also forcefully articulating a point. Short sentences can also be used to minimize an opponent's argument. Thus, you may draft a series of short, plain sentences when discussing an unfavorable precedent or detrimental fact. Longer, more descriptive sentences, in contrast, should be used to promote a warmer quality as they slow the reading pace and create a more favorable mood. Longer sentences may also be more effective when arguing equitable and policy considerations.

For the sake of clarity, most sentences should be simple. Judges are much more favorably disposed to arguments which they can grasp without having to read and reread. If you really understand the argument, you should be able to articulate it clearly and simply. Therefore, a sentence should contain only one main thought.

It is better to err in favor of too many short sentences because it is easier to combine simple sentences than to tear apart lengthy ones. In redrafting an overly long sentence, first isolate the main idea. State that idea as briefly and simply as possible. If necessary, modify or add to that idea by using additional short sentences.

Numerous techniques can be used to vary sentence structure. Dependent clauses (subject and verb which do not create a complete thought) can be introduced as an important idea which you want to impress upon the court:

> <u>Because Vitas' stock purchase did not involve a ''security'' within the meaning of the 1934 Act</u>, he has failed to allege all the requisite elements of a federal securities cause of action.

A dependent clause can be used effectively to convey an idea related to the main thought in the sentence:

> <u>Unlike the passive investor who must rely on others for critical information</u>, the majority purchaser is in a much better position to safeguard his investment and does not need the further protections afforded by the securities laws.

The dependent clause can also be used as a technique to advance a detrimental argument which is then refuted in the remainder of the sentence:

> <u>While the predicate offenses listed in the statute are not committed exclusively by members of organized crime</u>, most of them are offenses which traditionally have been strongly associated with organized crime syndicates.

Phrases can be used in a variety of ways to add color to a sentence. Phrases generally serve as an introductory device:

> <u>In light of Congress' express intent</u>, the sale of business doctrine correctly defines the type of investor the securities laws were designed to reach.

Phrases can be used to qualify the main thought in a sentence or to link the present sentence with the one immediately preceding it:

> The record indicates that all the parties knew they were dealing with ''stock'' and were acquainted with the characteristics of that instrument. <u>Under these circumstances</u>, Petitioner's expectation of securities law protection was entirely justified.

Sometimes a series of phrases can be used to list a series of conditions or to list several actions that a party has taken. When you are using this technique, make sure to use parallel structure for each phrase. Changing the structure makes the sentence confusing and difficult to read. In the following example, the writer did *not* use parallel structure:

> Their mission was to explore strange new worlds, to seek out new life and new civilizations, and boldly going where no man had gone before.

Punctuation can also be used to provide variety and enhance persuasion. A comma has the effect of slowing the pace of the reading, in much the same way as a speaker pauses while talking. A semicolon can be used to join together two short sentences into a single compound sentence. It is a useful technique to move the reader rapidly through similar facts touching upon the same topic:

> The Thirteenth Circuit Court of Appeals has followed that line of cases which incorrectly reads the Forman opinion as being first a ''literalist'' test and then an ''economic reality'' examination; it subsequently has applied the Howey test as the ''economic reality'' and found the shares of Wholesale Computer not to be securities in the requisite sense.

The semicolon also can be used when coupled with a conjunction or adverb to weaken or strengthen a thought. The colon is normally used to introduce a list or to set off ideas necessarily implied in words earlier in the sentence:

> RICO's language hardly could be more straightforward. There are only three elements necessary for a valid RICO claim under § 1964(c): (1) A violation of § 1962; (2) an injury to business or property; and, (3) a causal connection between the violation and the injury.

Certain persuasive devices are best used infrequently, if at all. These include exclamations, rhetorical questions, parentheses, and underlining, italics, boldface print, or capitalization for effect. The persuasiveness of the argument should result from effective legal analysis and persuasive writing, not from artificial signals denoting intended effect.

Overuse of these techniques decreases the persuasiveness of the writing. Too much emphasis is no emphasis. For a good example of short and plain writing, achieving clarity, brevity, and effective use of varying sentence length, read Lincoln's Gettysburg Address. It is only ten sentences long.

D. PERSUASIVE USE OF WORDS

The proper choice, use, and positioning of words in a sentence can help articulate arguments and direct the court's attention to the ideas being advanced. Avoid words that have several meanings unless the intended meaning is clear. A word such as "sanction," for example, has several meanings.

> `The rule sanctions this behavior by the attor-`
> `ney.`

Does the rule punish or allow this type of behavior? The use of a different word or the addition of an explanation will help avoid confusion as to your meaning.

While variety may add to the readability of a brief, exactness often demands repeating the same term to express the same idea. For example, if you first write that a court "held" something and later write that a court "said" something else, does that imply that the second statement by the court carries less weight than the first statement?

Be aware of the emotional tone which words convey. For example, "allege," "assert," and "declare" all have substantively similar meanings, but the emotional qualities of "allege" are defensive, while "assert" and "declare" connote positive, forceful, and direct qualities. Other sets of words with similar meanings but which convey distinctly different emotional qualities are "agree/admit," "avoid/evade," and "difference/discrepancy."

Some words carry harsh or even disparaging or pejorative qualities. Some examples are "attack," "quash," or "scheme." Overuse will diminish their effect and may even cause the court to sympathize with the opponent as the victim of a verbal attack and overstatement. A thesaurus will aid in finding synonyms with different emotional shadings, and can also be used to prevent unseemly repetition of words throughout the brief.

Be particularly attentive to grammatical rules and use plain, correct English. The brief is a formal document. Slang and vernacular terms should be avoided as creating an informal mood which is inconsistent with the brief's purpose. Legal sounding words such as "assume arguendo," "ergo," "aforementioned" and "said" seem pretentious and may also distract the judge's attention from the arguments in the brief. Overusing the words "clear," "clearly," and "certainly" may cause the judge to conclude that the writer lacks support for that proposition.

Keep the terms clear. Often, using the terms "appellant/appellee" or "petitioner/respondent" can lead to confusion as to exactly which party the writer is referring to in any given passage. Using the party's names may reduce confusion. Similarly, references to "the court" may be clarified by referring to the case name, such as "The *Howey* Court."

Sexism and using gender-specific pronouns are constant problems. There are several alternatives to using the pronoun "he" throughout the brief. These include: 1) use of a neutral word; 2) repeating the noun; 3) using both "he" and "she"; 4) alternating "he" and "she"; 5) using the form "s/he"; and, 6) rewriting to avoid the problem. Further suggestions for avoiding sexism are contained in Appendix D.

Some final suggestions:

1. Avoid double negatives. For example, in the following sentence, what is the writer trying to say?

   ```
   It is doubtful that the court would not have
   the power to impose this limitation.
   ```

2. Avoid redundancy, especially in the use of modifiers and negatives.

Avoid	*Use*
not inconsistent	consistent
not unreasonable	reasonable
true facts	facts
literal truth	truth
irregardless	regardless

3. Don't use a phrase when one word will do.

Avoid	*Use*
Due to the fact that	Because
Notwithstanding the fact	Although

4. Use care in using the words "that," "here," and "it." For example, the writer has overused "that" in the following sentence:

   ```
   The court held that, if the intent was to be
   given effect, in light of the legislative his-
   tory, that the statute should apply in this
   case.
   ```

A clearer version would be:

```
The court held that, in light of the Congres-
sional intent and the legislative history,
the statute should apply in this case.
```

Such errors will be more obvious if the sentence is read out loud.

Avoid	*Use*
There are few states that have	Few states have
It has been held by this court	This court has held
It is the belief of the respondent	Respondent believes

E. STRUCTURING PARAGRAPHS IN THE BRIEF

A paragraph is composed of three elements: an introduction, the development of the topic, and a conclusion. Each paragraph deals with only one discrete topic. When structuring a paragraph, construct an argument which leads the court logically to the desired conclusion, without distracting the court with tangential arguments or issues. Richard Lanham, in *Revising Prose,* suggests rewriting each paragraph in summary when revising a draft. If the paragraph cannot be written in one sentence, the paragraph likely contains too many ideas.

The introduction of the paragraph should clearly signify a shift or transition from the previous paragraph to a new phase of the contention being developed. The relationship between the previous paragraph and the new topic must be clarified and linked in the introduction of the new paragraph through the use of a transitional device.

One transitional device is a connecting word, such as "thus," "accordingly," or "consequently," which links the ideas in the two paragraphs. (The use of transitional phrases has been directly correlated with high essay scores in studies analyzing essay writing skills.) A second technique is to repeat in the introductory sentence a key word or phrase from the immediately preceding paragraph. A third transitional device involves a reference in the introductory sentence to the topic discussed in the preceding paragraph. Each of these techniques creates a sense of continuity within the brief.

The body of the paragraph is devoted to developing the topic which has been introduced in the introductory sentence. The topic discussed in the body of the paragraph is built around the topic sentence, which is a clear and persuasive articulation of a subheading of the outline. Like the subheading it embodies, the topic sentence contains a single, discrete idea.

The topic sentence thus does not stand alone in the paragraph. If it is to have any persuasive effect upon the court, the subpoint articulated in the topic sentence must be developed, supported, and expanded. The paragraph can be organized in either a deductive or inductive structure. To use the deductive method, place the topic sentence at the end of the paragraph, preceded by specific facts and supporting authorities from which the topic derives. To use the inductive method, state the topic sentence first, then develop it with specific examples. These methods of structuring the paragraph around the topic sentence should be varied throughout the brief to make the prose read in a more interesting and persuasive manner.

If writing inductively, complete the paragraph with a concluding sentence which reiterates the topic discussed in the body of the paragraph. The court should not be left with a dangling idea after reading the paragraph. The concluding sentence may also be used effectively to prepare the court for the following paragraph and its central theme.

Paragraph length, like sentence length is inversely correlated with readability. Take care not to bore the court with long and ponderous discussions of a single subpoint. Paragraphs generally should not extend more than one-half page in length. Abnormally lengthy paragraphs often indicate that more than one discrete subpoint is being discussed. In that case, the paragraph should be restructured into two paragraphs, each dealing with only one subpoint.

Paragraph length can be used to pace the court. Shorter paragraphs tend to speed up the judge's reading pace, while more lengthy paragraphs cause the judge to move more slowly through the argument. Thus, it is advantageous not to structure the brief with paragraphs of uniform length. Subpoints involving ideas incidental to the argument should be contained in shorter paragraphs, moving the judge more quickly through the development of these ideas. However, ideas fundamental to the contention should be treated in more lengthy paragraphs, forcing the court to spend greater time in reasoning through these more important topics.

If a complex, detailed and technical issue within the structure of one or more lengthy paragraphs must be argued, try concluding the final paragraph with a series of short and direct sentences phrased in the active voice. After reading the mass of substantive analysis in the paragraph, the judge may not pay close attention to a lengthy concluding sentence. If the conclusion is phrased in short sentences, however, it will catch the attention of the judge and demonstrate that the simple rationale embodied in the conclusion underlies the complex analysis.

IV. PRESENTING THE ARGUMENT

A. PERSUADING THE COURT

Keep in mind that appellate court judges and their law clerks are generally well-versed in the law. They are skilled in the reasoning process and sophisticated in their ability to perceive logical inconsistencies in superficially sound arguments. Never underestimate the intellectual capacities of the court.

A court must be informed before it can be convinced. Do not be so intent on persuading the court that you leap over the threshold step of making clear exactly what the complaint is, how it came about, and what you want the court to do about it. Despite their skills, appellate court judges may be unfamiliar with the specific area of the law upon which a legal strategy rests. Judges are most likely generalists, not specialists. Until informed, the court is likely to know nothing of the specific facts of the case on appeal.

Remember that judges are human beings. They can be moved by eloquent arguments and clear evidence of injustice, or they can be bored by dull, unimaginative writing. If a brief is not written in clear and simple fashion that allows the judge to understand without having to reread a paragraph a number of times to determine what is meant, the brief has failed in its purpose.

Courts of appeal generally have as their objective a fair and just result consistent with established legal principles. A brief therefore must contain three components: the facts of the case, the legal principles bearing on those facts, and the equitable consequences resulting from combining the facts and the law. Put yourself in the position of the judges. What do they want and expect from the brief? Judges want to know whether a decision, one way or the other, will be fair and just to the parties and in the public interest as well.

Remember the goal is to convince the court. You want the judge to think that your client has a good case, not merely to be impressed with how well you write. There is no better impression to leave than to have the judge say, "I understand what the advocate said. I have confidence in what the advocate said. I am persuaded by it and I am compelled to rule for his client."

B. COMBINING FACTS AND LAW

Legal precedents are worthless standing alone; their value lies in applying those precedents to the facts of your case to support your position. Courts decide cases based on the application of legal principles to the particular facts of the case, not on legal principles in the abstract. The following example from Petitioner's brief in the *Vitas* case shows how the facts of the case can be applied to a test prescribed by a previous decision:

> Vitas satisfies the Howey-Forman test. The Howey Court stated that a ''security'' exists when a person ''(1) invests his money in a common enterprise and (2) is led to expect profits (3) solely from the efforts of the promoter or a third party.'' 328 U.S. at 299; see also Forman, 421 U.S. at 852. In the present case, a common venture exists between Vitas and Madison, the other stockholder, because each contributed capital to the business. Cf. Frederikson, 637 F.2d at 1152 (''sharing or pooling funds'' satisfies common enterprise requirement). Furthermore, in light of Younger's statements regarding the

```
company's positive performance and Burton's
managerial success (R. 4-5), Vitas reasonably
expected to receive profits from his invest-
ment.
```

If the writer had merely stated the *Howey-Forman* test, the attempt to persuade the court that the test had been satisfied in this instance would have been far less effective. Applying facts to abstract legal principles not only clarifies the law, but demonstrates how the particular facts of the case fit within the body of established legal precedents.

C. PRESENTING FAVORABLE PRECEDENTS

In determining which cases are favorable, remember that few precedents ever directly apply to the facts of the case on appeal. The facts of the precedential cases must be carefully studied and compared to those of your case in order to show exactly how the two cases are similar and how they differ. Careful analysis will prevent you from presenting a case as "on point," only to have opposing counsel distinguish it, rendering it inapplicable.

Favorable precedents are handled in various ways depending upon their function. Generally, the greater the importance of the proposition being advanced, the greater the attention focused on the precedent which supports that proposition. If a precedential case supports a main proposition, don't just cite it; tell why the case, or line of cases applies. Mere citation of cases is an invitation to the court to examine the cases for themselves and ascertain their relevance to the point urged. This is a task which the judges may not have the time to undertake.

Every case relied on to support a main proposition should be analyzed. Provide the appellate tribunal with a terse statement of the facts of the precedent as they relate to the point for which the case is being cited. Then blend the reasoning of the holding with a favorable comparison between the facts of the precedent case and the facts of the case at bar. The reasoning of the holding may be demonstrated by a short quotation from the opinion. Given this analysis, the court will then be able, without outside research, to judge the extent to which the case relied on supports the contention.

Should you be fortunate enough to be in a position to choose from a number of favorable precedents, select the case from the highest court within that jurisdiction. If a state law principle is involved, select a state supreme court precedent. If no state supreme court precedent exists, use a precedent from the appellate court of the local jurisdiction. The same analysis holds true for federal courts when discussing federal law principles.

If the legal principle presented is adhered to in dozens of cases, it is sufficient to analyze only a few representative cases. Some others may then be cited. Select only those cases in which the factual pattern most closely resembles that of your case. If a rule of law has existed for a long time, point out not only that it has existed for many years, but also cite a recent case showing the continuing vitality of the rule.

When concluding the analysis of a precedent, direct the court to other cases which contain similar holdings, based on closely related facts. This is an effective and concise means of showing the court that the legal principles advanced are recognized in other jurisdictions and contexts. Do not analyze these concluding cases at length. Merely cite them and describe them briefly in parenthetical phrases so the court may investigate them if it wishes.

When providing additional cases, be careful not to string cite merely to demonstrate to the court the extent of your research. Long lists of citations are not a particularly effective method of persuasion, as judges may ignore what appears to be a mass of cases thrust upon them in this manner. Citing only one or two significant decisions following the analysis of an important and favorable precedent will often be far more effective than listing of similarly decided cases.

Courts often create explicit standards or tests to determine the outcome of cases. The most effective way to use the test is to articulate the holding and facts of the precedent, quote or paraphrase the test, and apply the facts of your case to show that each of the test's elements has been met. This technique reminds the court of the test to be applied, explains the factual context in which the test was originally created, and aids the court by applying the test to the facts under review. If the test to be applied is a lengthy one, it is usually preferable to paraphrase the test to make it more comprehensible rather than quoting it verbatim. In paraphrasing, include every essential element of the test.

It is proper to cite a case for favorable dicta if it is plainly labeled as such. In the absence of other authority to the contrary, judicial dicta may be deemed controlling. As with precedents, the persuasiveness of the dicta will depend on how closely the case from which it is drawn resembles your case in fact patterns and legal issues.

A dissenting opinion can also be cited to support an argument, particularly when the dissenting opinion itself presents a well-reasoned argument by a well-respected judge. Be sure to identify the citation from a dissenting opinion as a dissent. If the court believes that you are trying to conceal this fact, the court will lose faith in your other citations and arguments.

All points of law discussed in the brief, no matter how basic they may seem to be, should be supported by legal authority. When a precedent is used in support of a collateral point in the argument, however, it is sufficient to cite the case after articulating the point of law involved, without engaging in the more detailed analysis reserved for precedential supporting more important legal principles.

D. CONFRONTING UNFAVORABLE PRECEDENTS

Deal with unfavorable precedents in the same manner as favorable precedents—the more damning the precedent, the more effort you should expend distinguishing it. If the unfavorable precedent directly attacks or undermines a fundamental point in your argument you must disclose legal authority in the controlling jurisdiction known to be directly adverse to your position which is not disclosed by opposing counsel. Once it is presented, you are free to challenge its soundness. The unfavorable precedent will not go unnoticed if you fail to address it. By confronting the unfavorable precedent and distinguishing it in your brief, the precedent is much less damaging than it would be if it were discussed only in the opposition brief.

Unfavorable precedents which directly threaten a fundamental point in your argument can be dealt with in two ways. The easiest and most effective method of countering such unfavorable precedents is to distinguish their facts from those of your case. It is generally more effective and easier to distinguish an unfavorable precedent on its facts rather than argue that the case was erroneously decided. Demonstrate, for example, that, because the facts of the two cases are different, different legal principles apply to each factual situation.

The other way is to attack the precedent by showing that, while the same legal principles apply to both sets of facts, discrepancies between the two factual situations require that a different conclusion be drawn from the legal principle when applied to each case. If you maintain that the authority of a decision has been weakened, show that subsequent decisions have restricted its application or that changed conditions have rendered the precedent obsolete.

Directly attacking the validity of a holding is a less desirable means of dealing with an unfavorable precedent. Occasionally, however, courts will overrule existing authority and you must adopt this approach when no other path is open. One of two methods of attacking a precedent is usually employed. Either demonstrate that the precedent was decided incorrectly, pointing out flaws in the reasoning and analysis of the case, or attack the precedent by showing changed circumstances.

The latter means of discrediting an unfavorable precedent requires the advocate to examine the subsequent history of the holding in order to show that the underlying justification for the holding no longer exists. However, remember that courts are very reluctant to overrule cases. Therefore, consider a direct attack on the unfavorable precedent only when its facts cannot be distinguished.

E. EFFECTIVE PRESENTATION OF STATUTES

Statutes are employed in much the same manner as precedent cases to support an argument. If the statute clearly supports the point made, quote or paraphrase the statute. Apply the statute to the facts of the case to demonstrate how the case fits within the scope of the statute. It may also be necessary to define the terms of the statute either by reference to another statute or through a case interpreting the statute.

An effective way of employing statutes is to cite cases which are factually similar and have applied the statute favorably. Be sure to Shepardize these cases and the statute itself to insure that the interpretation of the statute has not been modified. This combination of statutory and case analysis provides a compelling foundation upon which to build an argument.

Statutes can also threaten legal arguments. An unfavorable statute is dealt with in a similar manner to that which is used to refute unfavorable precedents. The most successful method of discounting the effectiveness of an unfavorable statute is to show that the statute does not control the subject matter of the case, either because the statute relates to a different jurisdiction or because the statute governs conduct not relevant to the case.

If the unfavorable statute cannot be distinguished, either interpret the statute in a favorable manner or attempt to convince the court to void the statute. Voiding a statute usually requires an analysis showing that the unfavorable statute is in conflict with the applicable constitution. This is the least favored means of confronting an unfavorable statute. Unless the statute impinges upon a fundamental civil right or liberty, courts traditionally impose an almost irrefutable presumption in favor of a legislative enactment.

Attempting to reinterpret the statute is preferable to challenging its constitutionality. When the statute is drafted in ambiguous terms, you may be able to demonstrate to the court that the general rule of statutory construction requires you to search within the statute for its meaning. But when the language of the statute affords more than one interpretation, the legislative history and subsequent construction of the act may then be examined. In this manner, you may be able to develop an alternate interpretation of the statute which mitigates its previously unfavorable effect.

A resort to legislative history may be necessary even for favorable statutes when the statute is ambiguous or subject to various interpretations. This will be especially true when the particular statute has not been interpreted by the courts, or only has been interpreted by lower courts.

F. EFFECTIVE USE OF QUOTATIONS

Quotations from cited cases or statutes can be an effective means of showing legal support for a proposition. But remember that the purpose of the brief is to persuade the court with logically reasoned arguments, not to provide the court with a digest of applicable quotations. Remember that you are writing a *brief,* and not an explanatory text, article, or treatise.

One effective use of quotations is to provide an eloquent statement of a point of law which cannot be stated more persuasively or paraphrased. Quotations also can be used effectively to present a succinctly worded test which has been applied by past tribunals. Finally, quotations can be used to add emphasis to a heavily relied-upon precedent.

Misuse or ineffective use of quotations is less persuasive than not using any quotations at all. If the quotation is not reproduced verbatim, you must clearly indicate where changes have been made. In addition, quotations should never be used when they can be read out of context. Courts recognizing such misrepresentation will suspect all other quotations and citations.

Avoid lengthy quotations from opinions. Readers tend to skip the last part of a long indented quotation. Summarize lengthy passages, reproducing only those portions of the quote absolutely necessary to the brief. This will give your argument more authority than your own similarly worded language followed only by a citation. An exception to the rule against long quotations exists when the quotation is so clear and so well written that a paraphrasing would detract from its forcefulness.

Chapter Three

GENERAL RULES OF STYLE AND CITATION OF AUTHORITIES

Improper citation form and improper style intrudes upon the reader's attention, and distracts the reader from the arguments presented. Judges and their law clerks appreciate an advocate's use of proper citation form and style. It is therefore a matter of courtesy to the court and to the opposition to use proper citation form and style.

I. GENERAL RULES OF STYLE

A. ABBREVIATIONS

Abbreviations, although generally disfavored as inappropriately informal for brief writing, may be used in certain situations. Well-known statutes, agencies, or organizations may be designated by appropriate abbreviation or initials, once the full name has been presented and the proposed abbreviation introduced in parentheses:

```
Plaintiff's interpretation of the Racketeer
Influenced and Corrupt Organizations Act
(''RICO'')
```

Generally, abbreviations which require an apostrophe and the last letter of the abbreviated word are not followed by a period:

```
Ass'n, Dep't, Gov't, Nat'l
```

whereas abbreviations that do not use an apostrophe and do not use the last letter of the abbreviated word are followed by a period:

```
Co., Corp., Ry.
```

Widely recognized initials generally read as initials rather than as the words that they represent may be abbreviated using initials alone:

FTC, NLRB, UCLA

Initial abbreviations that are not read as initials require periods as do some exceptions to the rule concerning abbreviations of initials read as the words they represent:

N.Y., N.J., D.C.

Examples of abbreviations for reporters, codes and other authorities begin at page 65. Additionally, the proper citation form of an authority often may be found on the front page of the authority.

B. CAPITALIZATION

Capitalization is not always the subject of uniform rules and is often a matter left to the writer's discretion. Capitalization gives distinction, importance, and emphasis to words. Proper nouns are capitalized to signify the special importance of these words as the official names of particular persons, places and things. A number of words, however, may function as either proper or common nouns. Rules for capitalization of such terms as "petitioner" and "court" follow below.

1. Capitalizing Specific Words

The following words are capitalized only in the following situations:

"Act"—when part of a proper name given in full: Securities Exchange Act . . . the Act.

"Bill"—when part of a proper name given in full.

"Circuit"—when used with the circuit number: Ninth Circuit.

"Code"—when referring to a specific code: The 1939 and 1954 Tax Codes.

"Constitution"—when referring to the United States Constitution. *Exception:* federal constitution. Parts of the Constitution are not capitalized within a citation to the Constitution: article III, fifth amendment. U.S. Const. art. I. § 9, cl. 2, U.S. Const. amend. XIV, § 2, Exceptions: when using part of the Constitution as a proper noun, Bill of Rights, Commerce Clause, or First Amendment rights.

"Court"—when naming any court in full: The Supreme Court of California; *but,* this state's supreme court. The Court of Appeals for the Second Circuit or the Second Circuit Court of Appeals, *but,* the court of appeals. Always capitalize "Court" when referring to the United States Supreme Court. Also, when referring to the court to which the brief is being submitted, "Court" should be capitalized.

"Federal"—when the word it modifies is capitalized, and when discussing particular rules in the text of the brief: Federal Rules of Civil Procedure. However, "federal constitution" is not capitalized.

"Government"—when it is an unmodified noun standing alone meaning the United States government.

"Justice"—when referring to a Justice of the United States Supreme Court.

"National"—when the word it modifies is capitalized.

"Rule"—when part of a proper name given in full.

"Section"—only when used as a proper noun designation; *thus:* Congress chose to exempt small, private sales of stock from certain requirements under the Act but specifically applied the Section 10(b) antifraud provisions to all stock sales. The language of section 1964(c) of RICO and the language of section 4 of the Clayton Act, 15 U.S.C. § 15, are virtually identical.

2. Capitalizing Well-Known Statutes and Rules

The names of well-known statutes and rules, such as the Statute of Frauds and the Rule against Perpetuities, are customarily capitalized. Note, however, that "statute of limitations" is not capitalized.

3. Words Denoting Groups or Officeholders

Certain words are capitalized when used to refer to a specific group, officeholder, or government body. For example: the Agency, the Commission, the Congress, the Legislature, the President. On the other hand, these words are not capitalized when used as adjectives. For example, legislative decision, agency administration.

4. Title of Parties

Titles are often used to denote the parties to an action and serve two purposes. They remind the court of the procedural posture of the case by identifying which party brought the appeal, and they group a number of individual parties aligned on one side of an action. Thus, the terms Appellant, Appellee, Plaintiff, Defendant, Petitioner, and Respondent are capitalized when used to identify parties to the appeal. These terms, however, are never capitalized when referring to a party in another action (*i.e.*, in discussing the facts of an authority cited in the brief):

```
In that case, the court held that the peti-
tioner did have reasonable cause; similarly,
Petitioner in this case has reasonable cause
to believe unfair labor practices were com-
mitted.
```

5. Capitalizing Within Quotations

The first word of a quotation is usually capitalized to indicate distinctively and emphatically that a new sentence has begun. However, quotations are often most effective in a brief when they are woven into the context of a paragraph. In those cases, capitalization of the first word of the quotation will vary.

a. Quotation of a complete sentence following an introductory statement and a colon (whether the quotation is indented or not):

As this Court pointed out:

> We have emphasized in the recent past that
> ''[o]ur individual appraisal of the wisdom or
> unwisdom of a particular [legislative] course
> . . . is to be put aside in the process of in-
> terpreting a statute'' . . . .''

and

> As this Court pointed out: ''We have empha-
> sized in the recent past that '[o]ur individu-
> al appraisal of the wisdom or unwisdom of a
> particular [legislative] course . . . is to
> be put aside in the process of interpreting a
> statute' . . . .''

The first word of a quotation following a colon is capitalized when the quotation is intended to stand on its own as a complete sentence.

b. Quotation of less than a complete sentence following a colon which excludes the first portion of the sentence quoted:

> The Act provides that upon filing a petition:

> [T]he court . . . shall have jurisdiction to
> grant to the Board such temporary relief or
> restraining order as it deems just and proper.

Since the quotation follows a colon and is intended to stand on its own as a complete sentence, the first word must be capitalized. The first letter of the first word is capitalized and placed in brackets to indicate that in its original context it was not capitalized. Do not begin a quotation with an ellipsis (. . .).

c. Quotation of a complete sentence not intended to stand on its own as a complete sentence:

> As this Court has recognized, ''(t)he legis-
> lative history clearly demonstrates that the
> RICO statute was intended to provide new weap-
> ons of unprecedented scope for an assault upon
> organized crime and its economic roots.''

Although the first word of the quoted sentence is capitalized in its original form, the quotation has been woven into the text and is not intended to stand on its own. In the quotation, the first letter of the first word of the quotation is changed to a lower case letter and placed in brackets to indicate the change from its original form. Using a quotation in this manner can be very effective since a closer connection seems to be drawn by the interchangeability of language from the authority to the presentation of the case being argued.

d. Quotation of an incomplete sentence which includes the first word of the sentence:

> In <u>Weaver</u>, the Court noted that ''[e]ach transaction must be analyzed and evaluated on the basis of the content of the instruments in question . . . .''

In this context, although the first word of the quotation is capitalized in its original form, it is merely a clause within the textual sentence. As a result, the first letter has been changed to lower case and put in brackets to indicate the change. A quotation is used in this manner to show the exact wording.

e. Quotation of an incomplete sentence which does not include the first word of the sentence:

> In the instant case, Respondents ask the Court to evaluate the transaction ''on the basis of the content of the instruments in question . . . .''

In this context the quoted portion is merely used as a clause within a textual sentence. It is not intended to stand on its own and there have been no changes made. A quotation is used in this manner to show the exact language of the authority cited. The case on appeal and the authority cited are made to appear so closely related that the reasoning as well as language used in the cited authority may be used interchangeably with the case being argued to the court.

C. USING UNDERLINING IN LIEU OF ITALICS

Underlining in a typewritten brief is the counterpart to italics in a printed brief.

1. Case Names

The names of both parties and the *"v."* between them should be underlined with one continuous line. Underlining is also used in abbreviated references to cases in the text.

Thus:

> <u>United Housing Foundation, Inc. v. Forman</u>, 421 U.S. 837, <u>reh. denied</u>, 423 U.S. 884 (1975).

Hdbk.App. Advocacy 2nd Ed. ACB—3

Also:

In <u>Forman</u>, this Court found that the second prong of the test was not met.

All case names in a brief are underlined, including when they appear in a footnote.

Words indicating subsequent history are always underlined:

<u>Bennett v. Berg</u>, 685 F.2d 1053 (8th Cir.1982), <u>aff'd en banc</u>, 710 F.2d 1361 (8th Cir.1983).

2. *Introductory Signals*

All introductory signals are underlined (*"e.g.,"* *"see"* *"but see,"* *"see also"*). However, if any of these words are used in their ordinary sense rather than as a signal, they are not to be underlined.

3. *Foreign Words and Phrases*

Some foreign words always underlined *ex parte, ex rel., in re, inter alia, inter se, passim, quare, sic., sub nom.,* and *supra.*

Foreign words which are not underlined include ad hoc, a fortiori, amicus curiae, arguendo, bona fide, certiorari, de novo, dictum, ipso facto, mandamus, per curiam, per se, prima facie, pro rata, quo warranto, res judicata, stare decisis, and subpoena.

Foreign words may be more appropriate to academic writing generally than to brief writing. Pretentiousness and pedantism, permitted to the law professor in his domain, detracts from the persuasive task of the brief writer.

4. *Terms of Art*

When it is necessary to use terms of art, they should be enclosed in quotation marks to indicate the word or phrase has a special meaning given its context. In labor conflicts, for example, the phrase "dissolve and merge" has acquired a particular meaning:

Thus, it is evident that Smith & Jones is using the device of ''dissolve and merge'' as an economic weapon against the associates who have joined the union.

While terms of art may appear cumbersome in a sentence, they are useful to convey a precisely defined idea.

5. *To Provide Emphasis*

Underlining may be used to emphasize words or phrases in a quotation or in the text of the brief. This use of underlining is similar to using quotation marks to highlight a word or phrase in the text of a brief.

> If there are practical problems with RICO that Congress did not foresee, that would be an appropriate matter for <u>legislative</u> action.
>
> In <u>Forman</u> the Court stated: ''We perceive no distinction, <u>for present purposes</u>, between an 'investment contract' and an 'instrument commonly known as a security.''' <u>United Housing v. Forman</u>, <u>supra</u>, 421 U.S. at 853 (emphasis added).

Although the emphasis was provided in this instance, the advocate used the underlining portion to draw attention to the standard applied in the particular decision.

These techniques used to emphasize a word or phrase, are superficial and should be used sparingly. The brief should be written in such a way that the key words and phrases stand out without the aid of additional emphasis.

6. Headings

Underscoring is also used to identify and emphasize subheadings:

> 1. <u>Historically, corporate stock has been presumed covered by securities laws.</u>

As can be seen, underscoring the subheading distinguishes it from the body of the argument.

D. NUMBERS AND SYMBOLS

1. Numbers

Numbers from one to ten should be written out. Numbers over 100 should be expressed in figures. There are two accepted styles for expressing numbers greater than ten and less than 100. One style is to express such numbers in figures. Another style is to express them in words.

A brief is of a more formal and literary nature than is most journalism. Using figures can give numbers an undesired emphasis and obtrusiveness. Therefore, expressing numbers in words is generally used in briefs, except for references to statistical studies.

2. Symbols

When referring to dollars or percentages, the appropriate terms should be spelled out whenever the number is written (*thus:* fifty dollars, or thirty percent) and the appropriate symbol should be used when the arabic numerals are used (*thus:* $50,000, or 45%). There is no space between the symbols "$" and "%" and the numeral. Whether using words or numerals to express figures depends on the nature of the brief and the advocate's own style.

When referring to a particular section of an authority, the word "section," unless appearing as part of a full citation, should be used rather than merely a section sign (§).

> Under section 1964(c), ''any person'' injured by a violation of section 1962 ''shall recover threefold the damages he sustains . . . .''

But:

> ''Any person injured . . . by reason of a violation of section 1962 . . . shall recover threefold the damages he sustains . . . .''
> 18 U.S.C. § 1964(c) (1982).

When the "§" or "¶" sign is used, there should be a space between the sign and the numeral.

E. QUOTATIONS

Quotations may be used in a brief to emphasize the particular language of a court opinion or the language of an applicable statute. Because the exact wording is the primary reason a quotation is used, it should be accurate and clearly identified.

In the text of a brief, a quotation of three or more typographical lines may be indented and a quotation of over fifty words in length must be indented. Such indented quotations are not set off by quotation marks, and unless the applicable rules of court require otherwise, indented quotations are single-spaced. Indented quotations are usually preceded by a colon at the end of the textual sentence used to introduce the quotation.

> In <u>Landreth Timber Co. v. Landreth</u>, No. 81-3446, slip op. at 1315 (9th r. Mar. 7, 1984), the court stated:
>
>> We see no principled way to justify an analysis in which we determine whether a note is a ''security'' within the meaning of the Acts by examining the transaction in light of the statutory purpose.

Note that double quotation marks are used within an indented quotation.

Shorter quotations or quotations under fifty words may be incorporated into the regular flow of the sentence and may be set off by quotation marks. *Thus:*

```
Hence, the residents could not have been
''misled by use of the word 'stock' into be-
lieving that the federal securities laws gov-
erned their purchase.''  Forman, 421 U.S. at
851.
```

Note that the citations to the quotations in the two previous examples appear in different locations—one before the quotation, one after the quotation. The location of the citation is not determined by whether the quotation is indented or not; it depends on how it is being introduced.

The paragraph structure of a quotation is not indicated unless the quotation is indented (*i.e.,* over three lines or fifty words). Where the quotation is indented, the first sentence of each paragraph of the quotation is further indented to show the paragraph structure of the material quoted. Do not, however, indent the first sentence of the first paragraph unless the first word of the original paragraph is included in the quotation.

1. *Placement of Quotation Marks*

Periods and commas should always be placed inside quotation marks. However, when a word, short phrase, or the exact wording and sentence structure of a decision or statute is quoted, periods and commas are placed outside the quotation marks. *Thus:*

```
The definitions in the 1933 and 1934 Acts are
both preceded by the phrase, ''unless the con-
text otherwise requires.''  15 U.S.C. § 77b,
15 U.S.C. § 78c(a).
```

But:

```
RICO is designed to ''divest the association
of the fruits of its ill-gotten gains.''
United States v. Turkette, 452 U.S. 576, 585
(1981).
```

If you use a phrase for effect, not in relation to any specific authority, no citation is necessary. *Thus:*

```
This Court has indicated that if something is
called ''stock,'' then it should be consid-
ered a ''security.''
```

2. *Omissions from Quotations (Ellipsis)*

Omissions are indicated by insertion of three evenly spaced periods (ellipsis) set off by a space before the first and after the last period to take the place of the word or words omitted. This ellipsis signal should never be used to begin a quotation. While such editing reflects the advocate's own interpretation of what the source intended, the integrity of the source must not be threatened in the process.

a. Phrases or Clauses

No ellipsis is necessary when there is no omission within the quotation.

> The court in Moss noted that RICO was enacted to deal with the unlawful activities of those engaged in organized crime. The court then stated: ''The language of the statute, however, does not premise a RICO violation on proof or allegations of any connection with organized crime.'' Moss v. Morgan Stanley Inc., 719 F.2d 5, 21 (2nd Cir.1983).

However, an omission is indicated when it occurs within a quotation:

> The Second Circuit expressly noted that ''(t)he language of the statute . . . does not premise a RICO violation on proof . . . of any connection with organized crime.'' Moss, 719 F.2d at 21.

When the omission comes at the end of the quotation, it is not always indicated. When the quoted phrase or clause is in the middle of a textual sentence, the omission at the end of the quotation usually is not indicated.

> Specifically, this Court held that inclusion of this subject within the meaning of section 8(d) ''would promote the fundamental purpose of the Act'' and be conducive to industrial peace.

If, however, this quotation is used at the end of a textual sentence, an omission from the end of the quotation should be indicated.

> Specifically, this Court held that inclusion of this subject within the meaning of section 8(d) ''would promote the fundamental purpose of the Act . . . .''

Note, when the ellipsis signal appears at the end of the quoted sentence there is a space before the three periods, as usual. There is, however, no space between the last period of the ellipsis and the period indicating the end of the sentence. This variation in the rule clearly indicates not only the end of the quoted sentence, but the end of the textual sentence as well.

b. Quoted Sentences Intended to Stand on Their Own

If the quoted language is intended to stand by itself as a complete sentence, but the language beginning the original sentence has been deleted, capitalize the first letter of the remaining quoted portion and place it in brackets. An omission of language in the middle of a quoted sentence is indicated in the same manner as such omissions are indicated in a quoted phrase or clause. When deleting language at the end of a quoted sentence, insert the ellipsis between the last word and the period or final punctuation.

When language is deleted from the end of a quoted sentence and the beginning portion of the following quoted sentence, four spaced periods are used. Likewise, when an entire sentence is deleted from the middle of a quotation, the omission is indicated by four spaced periods. The first three periods indicate an omission from the end of the quoted sentence. The fourth period, being spaced rather than closed in, indicates that language following the ending punctuation in the original sentence has also been omitted. The four spaced periods are used only when the quotation continues beyond the omitted portion.

> The indication that the Board has jurisdiction and will likely exercise it, ... coupled with considerations of public policy and equity, require that a temporary injunction be issued to promote the goals of the Act.

If the omitted language comes after the end of a quoted sentence, but is followed by further quotation, the ending punctuation of the quoted sentence is retained. Depending on the amount of material omitted, a three or four-period ellipsis is inserted before the remainder of the quotation. Note that two spaces must intervene between the ending punctuation of the quoted sentence and the ellipsis.

> [J]urisdiction is asserted over all nonretail enterprises which have an <u>outflow or inflow</u> across State lines of at least $50,000, whether <u>such outflow or inflow be regarded as direct or indirect</u>. . . . adding direct and indirect outflow, or direct and indirect inflow. (Emphasis in original.)

Capitalization of the first letter of the remainder of the quotation following the period will depend on whether the remainder begins at the beginning of a new quoted sentence or whether the remainder can stand on its own. In both of these cases the first letter is capitalized, either by leaving it as it appears in the original sentence or changing it in a capital letter and placing it in brackets. Otherwise, the remainder begins with a lower case letter, as in the example.

c. Paragraphs

In an indented quotation, if the language at the beginning of the first paragraph of the quote is omitted, do not further indent the beginning of the quote. Indicate omissions in the beginning of subsequent paragraphs within the quote by beginning them with an indented ellipsis. Indicate omitted paragraphs by an indented ellipsis followed by a period:

> ```
> [W]e appreciate the concerns motivating the
> district court to limit RICO's scope . . . .
>
>     . . . The language of the statute, however,
> does not premise a RICO violation on proof or
> allegations of any connection with organized
> crime.
> ```

3. Alterations Within Quotations (Emphasis added.)

Alterations are made in a quotation to emphasize a particular point, to clarify the language of the quotation, or to omit material that is unnecessary or cumbersome.

a. Adding Emphasis

Indicate a quotation for emphasis by underlining some portion of the language of the quotation by placing a parenthetical statement at the end of and as part of the citation in the quotation. If the citation precedes the quotation, the parenthetical statement appears by itself at the end of the quotation. This parenthetical statement should indicate the nature of the change made to the quotation.

> ```
> ''[A] complaint should not be dismissed for
> failure to state a claim unless it appears be-
> yond doubt that the plaintiff would prove no
> set of facts in support of his claim which
> would entitle him to relief.'' Conley v. Gib-
> son, 355 U.S. 41, 45-46 (1957) (emphasis add-
> ed).
> ```

If portions of the quotation were italicized in their original context, this should be indicated in a similar fashion.

> ```
> [J]urisdiction is asserted over all nonretail
> enterprises which have an outflow or inflow
> across State lines of at least $50,000, wheth-
> er such outflow or inflow be regarded as di-
> ```

`rect` or indirect. 122 N.L.R.B. at 85 (emphasis in original).

b. Omitting Unnecessary or Cumbersome Material

Omitting footnotes or citations from a quotation is indicated by a parenthetical statement, "(citations omitted)" or "(footnotes omitted)," at the end of the quotation which reflects the nature of the omission. This type of material is often omitted because it interrupts the flow of the quotation in the context of the brief. Such references usually refer to material outside the scope and purpose for which the quotation was used.

*c. Clarifying of **Material** or Language Within the Quotation*

When the first letter of a word within a quotation must be changed, do so by placing the changed letter in brackets.

[It] is not possible to say whether a satisfactory solution could be reached . . . .

Also indicate inserted words replacing a noun or pronoun or changing the tense or number of a verb, by placing the inserted word or words in brackets.

The court described a RICO enterprise as:

an entity, for present purposes a group of persons associated together for a common purpose of engaging in a course of conduct. . . . [The enterprise] is proved by evidence . . . that the various associates function as a continuing unit.

Turkette, 452 U.S. at 583.

d. Citing Quoted Materials

The page on which a quotation begins and, if it continues to another page, the page on which it ends should be indicated (e.g. 609 F.2d at 303–304, 472 F.2d at 721–22). Even if the source of the quotation is indicated to introduce the quotation (*e.g.,* "In *Forman,* the court stated . . .") citation to where the quotation actually appears is indicated immediately following the quotation (*e.g.,* 421 U.S. at 787). The citation should be presented as an independent sentence following the quotation, or immediately following the name of the case.

F. FOOTNOTES

A writer should remember that the brief is to be written persuasively. You may have only a limited number of pages in which to present your argument. Before adding a footnote you should ask yourself if, since you do not consider the material important enough to put into the body of the brief, it should be included at all. Does it add to the persuasive nature of the argument? On the other hand, single-spaced footnotes may save you precious space.

Footnotes are never used in a brief for the citation of an authority. They may, however, be used to provide the reader with additional information, which may be of interest, without unnecessarily disrupting the flow of the brief. Analogous laws, authority from other jurisdictions, statistical information, and discussions of secondary authorities are items that are more appropriate in a footnote than in the text.

Footnotes are indicated by consecutive arabic numbers set off on a typewriter either by underlining the number and placing a slash after it "2/", or by raising the number above the text."2" Regardless of the method chosen, a footnote placed in the middle of a sentence is always followed by one space. Wherever a footnote indicated at the end of a sentence is placed immediately after the punctuation, it is followed by two spaces.

The footnote itself should appear at the bottom of the page on which the footnote indicator appears. A line should appear above the footnote to indicate that the material beneath the line is not part of the text. Additionally, the footnote should be preceded by an arabic number corresponding to that appearing in the text of the brief which must be typed in the same manner (i.e., "2/" or "2").

G. USING DASHES AND PARENTHETICALS

A detailed discussion of the proper use of punctuation is beyond the scope of this handbook. Students are advised to consult: L. Squires & M. Rombauer, *Legal Writing in a Nutshell* (1982); W. Irmscher, *The Holt Guide to English* (3d ed. 1981); *The Chicago Manual of Style* (13th ed. 1982); and, K. Turabian, *A Manual For Writers of Term Papers, Theses, and Dissertations* (4th ed. 1973), for a comprehensive discussion of the rules governing punctuation. Nevertheless, two punctuation marks deserve special attention: the dash, because of its seldom but effective use; and the parenthesis, because of its common but often incorrect use.

Although the dash has a few specific functions, it most often serves in place of the comma, the semicolon, the colon, or parenthesis. When used as an alternative to these marks, it creates a much more emphatic separation of words within a sentence. Because of its versatility, careless writers are tempted to use a dash to punctuate almost any break within a sentence. However, the indiscriminate use of dashes is not only inappropriate, but will only serve to destroy the special forcefulness of this mark. Hence, use the dash infrequently—and then only for deliberate effect.

The dash is constructed by placing two hyphens together with no space before, between, or after the hyphens. The dash should always follow a word and should never be used to begin a new line.

Parentheses and dashes serve many of the same functions, but they differ in one significant respect. Parentheses can set off only nonessential elements, whereas dashes can set off essential and nonessential elements. In setting off material, dashes emphasize; parentheses de-emphasize.

Parentheses should not be used to include additional, unnecessary information. Generally, if the information cannot be worked into the text, then it probably does not belong in the text. If the information to be put in parentheses is important but lengthy, consider placing it in a footnote.

Parentheses enclose explanatory material which is independent of the main thought of the sentence. Use parenthetical explanations when dashes would be too emphatic and commas would be inappropriate or confusing. The parentheses should enclose only what is truly parenthetical, and not words or phrases essential to the construction of the sentence.

When using parentheses, be sure that the punctuation is in the correct location. If the parenthetical is within a sentence, then the punctuation should fall outside of the closing parenthesis. If, however, the parentheses contain a full sentence, then the punctuation should go inside the last parenthesis.

H. REFERENCE WORDS

1. *"Infra"*

Although the term *"infra"* is frequently used in other scholarly works, it should not be used in a brief. Using *"infra"* refers the reader to a subsequent point in the brief, thereby ignoring the logical progression which an advocate has painstakingly developed as the most persuasive order of presentation.

2. *"Supra"*

The term *"supra"* is commonly used in other scholarly works to refer the reader to material previously mentioned in the discussion. But in brief writing, the use of *"supra"* is both unwarranted and unwise. Technically, *"supra"* tells the reader to look elsewhere in the brief for the missing information. This can only serve to annoy the reader (by causing him to thumb through the pages of the brief in search of the material), and interrupt his train of thought.

3. "Id."

The reference word "*id.*" is used in a brief when citing to the immediately preceding authority. It may be used in citing to any kind of authority, and should only be used when it is clear to the reader to which authority you refer. "Id." cannot be used if there has been an intervening authority. Moreover, if the reference to the particular authority is separated by several pages from that authority, the writer should provide the reader with the full citation, since causing the reader to thumb through the brief in search of the authority can only serve to disrupt the persuasive flow of the argument.

When using the reference word "*id.*", the writer should always include the page on which the information can be found. (i.e., *id.* at 433.) If, however, the material is contained on the same page as that indicated by the previous citation, then the writer need not include the page number. Additionally, if "*id.*" is used within a sentence, then the first letter of the reference word is not capitalized. It is only when "*id.*" is the first word of a sentence that the "*i*" is capitalized.

There is no categorical rule regarding the number of cases that should be cited. The writer should use discretion, citing no more than two or three cases from the same jurisdiction for the same proposition of law, unless it is the main issue of the case. In any event, a writer faced with a great deal of authority pertaining to the same proposition of law may wish to cite to the earliest or most famous case, and a recent case to emphasize its continuing validity.

I. REFERENCES TO OTHER DOCUMENTS

1. *The Record*

In an appellate brief, every assertion of fact must be supported by a reference to the page, or pages, in the record where the supporting testimony can be found. This provides the reader with a means of verification and demonstrates to the reader that the assertions are something more than mere rhetoric.

The reference to the record should immediately follow the assertion of fact. Such citations are placed in parentheses with a capital letter "R." and the page number of the record where the information can be found (R. 69). The record reference is considered part of the sentence, and as such, *precedes* the sentence punctuation.

2. *The Brief*

Just as an assertion of fact must be supported by a citation to the record, a reference to material contained in an opponent's brief must be supported by a citation to that brief.

If referring to a brief which has been filed in the pending appeal, then an advocate need only use the designation given on the brief itself, and identify the page on which the information can be found:

''Brief for Appellant at 7.''

If, on the other hand, the advocate is referring to a brief filed in a previous action, then he must use the designation given on the document itself, followed by a full citation to the case to which it relates:

''Brief for Respondent at 7, Lino v. City Investing Co., 487 F.2d 689 (3d Cir.1973)''

''Brief for Appellant at 8-12, United States v. Anderson, 626 F.2d 1358 (8th Cir.1980), cert. denied, 450 U.S. 912 (1980)''

A short form of the case name may be used, or the case name may be omitted, if the reference would be clear and unambiguous to the reader.

3. *The Appendix*

If there is an appendix to the brief, citation to it will depend upon how the appendix is organized. When the appendices are lettered separately, refer to the letter of the appendix. Thus: "Appendix B." If the reference is to a particular page of a general appendix, then cite as follows: "Appendix at p. 6." The appendices are paginated independently of the pagination provided for the brief. This gives the reader a clear indication when the text ends and the appendix begins.

II. CITATION

An effective brief must give correct and complete citations. The citations must be given in their proper order and contain all necessary information. The purpose of the citation is to cite the authority for the statement or position taken in the brief and to allow the reader of the brief to go directly to the same source.

The following section is not intended to be an exhaustive discussion of proper citation. There are already several sources in the field governing citation style. Aside from governing a particular jurisdiction, the most widely used citation system is contained in *A Uniform System of Citation*, Thirteenth Edition (commonly referred to as "The Blue Book"). The following section is intended only to supplement and to clarify The Blue Book by providing a table of unofficial and topical reporter citations in Roman type.

A. CASES

1. General Information

a. Procedural Phrases

Abbreviate "on the relation of," "for the use of," "on behalf of," and similar expressions to "*ex rel.*" Abbreviate "in the matter of," "petition of," and similar expressions to "*in re.*" Omit all procedural phrases except the first. When adversary parties are named, omit all procedural phrases except "*ex rel.*"

b. State Names

"State of," "Commonwealth of," and "People of" are omitted except when citing decisions to a court sitting in the state which is identified as a party to the action. In that instance, only "State," "Commonwealth," or "People" should be retained. For example, cite *State v. Swanson* to a court sitting in Minnesota. The same case is cited as *Minnesota v. Swanson* to a court sitting outside of Minnesota.

c. Case History

The subsequent history of the case becomes a part of the citation whenever the case is cited in full. If the date of the subsequently published history is printed in the same year as the opinion cited, the date is indicated only at the end of both citations. Prior history should be given as part of the citation only if significant to a point for which the case is cited. Examples follow:

```
Darlington Manufacturing Co. v. NLRB, 397
F.2d 760 (4th Cir.1968), cert. denied, 393
U.S. 1023 (1969).
```

```
Masonite Corp. v. International Woodworkers
of America, AFL-CIO, 215 So.2d 691 (Miss.),
cert. denied, 394 U.S. 974 (1968).
```

```
Clinton v. Commonwealth, 204 Va. 275 (1963),
rev'd per curiam sub nom., Clinton v. Virgin-
ia, 377 U.S. 158 (1964).
```

2. United States Supreme Court Cases

The official reporter is the *United States Reports* (U.S.). The unofficial reporters are the *Supreme Court Reporter* (S.Ct.) and the *Lawyer's Edition* (L.Ed.). Recent decisions can also be found in the *United States Law Week* (U.S.L.W.). For brief writing purposes, citation to the official reporter is all that is required. A parallel citation need not be given.

If the official reporter containing the decision has not yet been published, then the advocate should cite to the *Supreme Court Reporter* or, if not therein, to the *United States Law Week.* Citation to these unofficial reporters will indicate that the case cannot, as yet, be found in the official reporter. Therefore, this fact need not be indicated separately in the brief by using "___ U.S. ___."

Examples follow.

Goldfarb v. Virginia State Bar, 421 U.S. 773 (1975).

Goldfarb v. Virginia State Bar, 95 S.Ct. 2004 (1975).

Goldfarb v. Virginia State Bar, 44 L.Ed.2d 572 (1975).

NLRB v. Local Union No. 103, 46 U.S.L.W. 4081 (January 17, 1978).

3. *Other Federal Cases*

a. *Official Reporters*

Lower federal court decisions may be found in several sources. These are, primarily, the *Federal Reporter, Federal Supplement, Federal Rules Decisions,* and the *Bankruptcy Reporter.*

Examples follow.

Brown v. Pacific Telephone and Telegraph Co., 218 F.2d 542 (9th Cir.1954).

International Ladies' Garment Workers Union v. NLRB, 463 F.2d 907 (D.C.Cir.1972).

Johnston v. Evans, 223 F.Supp. 766 (E.D.N.C. 1963).

Dooley v. Highway Truckdrivers and Helpers Local 107, 192 F.Supp. 198 (D.Del.1961).

Computer Network Corp. v. Spohler, 95 F.R.D. 500 (D.D.C.1982).

In re Standard Furniture, 3 B.R. 527 (Bankr. S.D.Cal.1980).

B. TOPICAL REPORTERS AND SERVICES

When a lower federal court decision has not been reported in an official reporter, either because it is too recent or because the case has not been chosen for publication, it may appear in one of the unofficial topical reporters. In that case the topical reporter should be cited. The proper abbreviation for these topical reporters is:

Administrative Law Reporter Second (¶) . . . . . . Ad.L.2d (P & F)

All State Sales Tax Reporter (¶) . . . . All State Sales Tax
Rep. (CCH)

American Stock Exchange Guide (page) . . . . . . Am.Stock Ex. Guide
(CCH)

Antitrust & Trade Regulation Report (page and
section letter) . . . . Antitrust & Trade Reg.
Rep. (BNA)

Atomic Energy Law Reporter (¶) . . . . Atom.En.L.Rep. (CCH)

Automobile Law Reporter (¶) . . . . Auto.L.Rep. (CCH)

Automobile Insurance Cases (¶) . . . . Auto.Ins.Cas. (CCH)

Aviation Law Reporter (¶) . . . . Av.L.Rep. (CCH)

 Aviation Cases . . . . Av.Cas.

Bankruptcy Law Reporter (¶) . . . . Bankr.L.Rep. (CCH)

Blue Sky Law Reporter (¶) . . . . Blue Sky L.Rep. (CCH)

Commodity Futures Law Reporter (¶) . . . . Comm.Fut.L.Rep. (CCH)

Conditional Sale—Chattel Mortgage Reporter
(page) . . . . Condit.Sale—Chat.Mort.
Rep. (CCH)

Consumer Credit Guide (¶) . . . . Cons.Cred. Guide (CCH)

Consumerism (page and ¶, in different sections) Consumerism (CCH)

Corporation Guide (¶) . . . . Corp. Guide (P–H)

Corporation Law Guide (¶) . . . . Corp.L. Guide (CCH)

Cost Accounting Standards Guide (¶) . . . . Cost Acc'g Stand.
Guide (CCH)

Criminal Law Reporter (page) . . . . Crim.L.Rep. (BNA)

Economic Controls (¶) . . . . Econ.Cont. (CCH)

Employment Practices Guide . . . . Empl.Prac. Guide (CCH)

 Employment Practices Decisions . . . . Emp.Prac.Dec.

Energy Users Report (page and section letter) En. Users Rep. (CCH)

Environment Reporter (page) . . . . Envir.Rep. (BNA)

Equal Employment Opportunity . . . . EEOC Comm.Man.
 Commission Compliance Manual (¶) . . . . . . (CCH)

Family Law Reporter (page) . . . . Fam.L.Rep. (BNA)

 bound in same name . . . . Fam.L.Rep.

Federal Banking Law Reporter (¶) . . . . Fed. Banking L.Rep.
(CCH)

Federal Carriers Reporter (¶) . . . . Fed.Carr.Rep. (CCH)

 Federal Carriers Cases . . . . Fed.Carr.Cas.

Federal Estate and Gift Tax Reporter (¶) . . . . . Fed.Est. & Gift **Tax**
Rep. (CCH)

Federal Excise Tax Reporter (¶) . . . . Fed.Ex. Tax Rep. **(CCH)**

Federal Securities Law Reporter (¶) . . . . Fed.Sec.L.Rep. (CCH)

Federal Taxes (¶) . . . . Fed. Taxes (P–H)

Federal Taxes Estate and Gift Taxes (¶) . . . . . . Fed. Taxes Est. & Gift
(P–H)

Federal Taxes Excise Taxes (¶) . . . . Fed. Taxes Excise
(P–H)

Food Drug Cosmetic Law Reporter (¶) . . . . Food Drug Cos.L.Rep.
                                                      (CCH)

Government Contracts Reporter (¶) . . . . Govt.Cont.Rep. (CCH)
    Board of Contract Appeals Decisions . . . . . . Govt.Cont.Rep. (CCH)
    Contract Cases, Federal . . . . Cont.Cas.Fed.

Government Employee Relations Report (page
    and section letter) . . . . Govt.Empl.Rel.Rep.
                                                      (BNA)

Housing & Development Reporter (page) . . . . . . Hous. & Dev.Rep.
                                                      (BNA)

Industrial Relations (¶) . . . . Ind.Rel. (P–H)

Insurance Law Reporter (page) . . . . Insur.L.Rep. (CCH)
    Automobile Cases 2d Auto.Cas.2d
    Fire & Casualty Cases . . . . Fire & Casualty Cas.
    Life (Health, Accident) Cases 2d . . . . Life Cas.2d
    Negligence Cases 2d Negl.Cas.2d

Labor Arbitration Awards (¶) . . . . Lab.Arb. Awards (CCH)
    bound in same name . . . . Lab.Arb. Awards

Labor Arbitration Service . . . . Lab.Arb.Serv. (P–H)

Labor Law Reporter (¶) . . . . Lab.Rep. (CCH)
    Labor Cases . . . . Lab.Cas.
    NLRB Decisions . . . . NLRB Dec.

Labor Relations Reporter . . . . Lab.Rel.Rep. (BNA)
    Fair Employment Practices Cases . . . . Fair Empl.Prac.Cas.
    Labor Arbitration and Dispute Settlements Lab.Arb. & Disp.Sett.
    Labor Relations Reference Manual . . . . L.R.R.M.
    Wage and Hour Cases . . . . Wage and Hour Cas.

Mutual Funds Guide (¶) . . . . Mut.Funds Guide (CCH)

New York Stock Exchange Guide (page) . . . . . . NYSE Guide (CCH)

Pension Plan Guide (¶) . . . . Pens.Plan Guide (CCH)

Poverty Law Reporter (¶) . . . . Pov.L.Rep. (CCH)

Private Foundations Reporter (¶) . . . . Priv.Found.Rep. (CCH)

Products Liability Reporter (¶) . . . . Prod.Liab.Rep. (CCH)

Public Utilities Report (¶) . . . . Pub.U.Rep. (PUR)

Radio Regulation (¶) . . . . Rad.Reg. (P–H)

Securities Regulation & Law Report (page and
    section letter) . . . . Sec.Reg. & L.Rep.
                                                      (BNA)

Securities Regulation Guide (¶) . . . . Sec.Reg. Guide (P–H)

Selective Service Law Reporter (page and ¶, in
    different sections) . . . . Sel.Serv.L.Rep. (PLEI)

Standard Excess Profits Tax Reporter (¶) . . . . . Stand.Ex.Prof. Tax Rep.
                                                      (CCH)

Standard Federal Tax Reporter (¶) . . . . Stand.Fed.Tax Rep.
                                                      (CCH)

        U.S. Tax Cases . . . . U.S. Tax Cas.

State and Local Taxes (¶ by section) . . . . State & Loc. Taxes
                                                      (BNA)

State Motor Carrier Guide (¶) . . . . State Mot.Carr. Guide (CCH)

State Tax Cases Reporter (¶) . . . . State Tax Cas.Rep. (CCH)

State Tax Cases . . . . State Tax Cas.

Tax Court Reported Decisions (page) . . . . Tax Ct.Rep.Dec. (P–H)

Tax Court Reporter (decision number) . . . . Tax Ct.Rep. (CCH)

Tax Court Memorandum Decisions (page) . . . . . Tax Ct.Mem.Dec. (CCH)

bound in same name . . . . Tax Ct.Mem.Dec.

Tax Exempt Organizations (¶) . . . . Tax Exempt Orgs. (CCH)

Tax Management (section number) . . . . Tax Mngmt. (BNA)

Trade Regulation Reporter (¶) . . . . Trade Reg.Rep. (CCH)

Unemployment Insurance Reporter (¶ within section) . . . . Unempl.Ins.Rep. (CCH)

United States Law Week (page) . . . . U.S.L.W.

United States Patent Quarterly (page) . . . . U.S.P.Q. (BNA)

Urban Affairs Reporter (¶) . . . . Urb.Aff.Rep. (CCH)

Utilities Law Reporter (¶) . . . . Util.L.Rep. (CCH)

Workmen's Compensation Law Reporter (¶) . . . Workmen's Comp.L.Rep. (CCH)

Wills, Estates, Trusts (¶) . . . . Wills, Est., Tr. (P–H)

C. ADMINISTRATIVE BOARDS

Decisions of administrative boards, like court decisions, should be cited to the official report if the case is included there. If the official report of a decision has not yet been bound and paginated, citation should be by case number and include the full date of the decision. In such cases, citation should be to an official release, and, whenever possible, a parallel citation to an unofficial reporter or service should be provided so that the court can more easily locate the opinion. In the text of the brief, either citation, or both, may be used. The following is a list of official administrative reporters:

Administrative Decisions under Immigration and Nationalization Laws	1940–date	I. & N. Dec.
Agricultural Decisions	1942–date	Agric.Dec.
Atomic Energy Commission Reports	1956–1975	A.E.C.
Civil Aeronautics Board Reports (Vol. 1 by C.A.A.)	1940–date	C.A.B.
Copyright Decisions	1909–date	Copy.Dec.
Court of Customs Appeals Reports	1919–1929	Ct.Cust.App.
Cumulative Bulletin	1919–date	C.B.
Customs Bulletin and Decisions	1967–date	Cust.B. & Dec.
Decisions of the Comptroller General	1921–date	Comp.Gen.
Decisions of the Employees' Compensation Appeals Board	1947–date	Empl.Comp.App.Bd.

Decisions of the Department of the Interior	1881–date	Interior Dec.
Decisions of the Federal Maritime Commission	1947–date	Dec.Fed.Mar.Comm'n
Decisions of the United States Maritime Commission	1919–1947	Dec.U.S.Mar.Comm'n
Department of the Interior, Decisions Relating to Public Lands	1881–date	Pub. Lands Dec.
Federal Communications Commission Reports	1934–date	F.C.C.
Federal Power Commission Reports	1981–date	F.P.C.
Federal Reserve Bulletin	1915–date	Fed.Res.Bull.
Federal Trade Commission Decisions	1915–date	F.T.C.
Interstate Commerce Commission Reports	1931–date	I.C.C.
Interstate Commerce Commission Valuation Reports	1929–date	I.C.C. Valuation Rep.
Motor Carrier Cases	1936–date	M.C.C.
National Labor Relations Board Decisions and Orders	1935–date	N.L.R.B.
National Railroad Adjustment Board, 1st–4th Div.	1934–date	*e.g.,* N.R.A.B. (1st Div.)
National Transportation Safety Board Decisions	1967–date	N.Trans.S.Dec.
Official Gazette of the United States Patent Office		Off.Gaz.Pat. Office
Official Opinions of the Solicitor for the Post Office Department	1878–1951	Op.Solic.P.O. Dep't
Opinions of the Attorney General	1789–date	Op.Att'y Gen.
Patents, Decisions of the Commissioner and of U.S. Courts	1869–date	Dec.Com.Pat.
Securities and Exchange Commission Decisions and Reports	1934–date	S.E.C.
Treasury Decisions Under Customs and Other Laws	1943–date	Treas.Dec.
Treasury Decisions Under Internal Revenue Laws	1942	Treas.Dec.Int.Rev.

D. STATE CASES

An advocate should cite state court cases to the official reporter as well as to the unofficial reporter. If the state does not have an independent official reporter, then the unofficial reporter must be cited alone. The following states do not presently have independent official state reporters: Alaska, Florida, Mississippi, Missouri, North Dakota, Oklahoma, Texas, and Wyoming.

In some jurisdictions the decisions of the various appellate levels are reported in a single reporter. In these cases, the advocate must indicate the particular court which rendered the decision. Unless the court is expressly indicated, the implication is that the court rendering the decision is the highest court in the state.

Where the case has not yet been published in either an official or unofficial reporter, the case should be cited by its docket number, the court rendering the decision, and the full date of the decision. The following list compiles the abbreviations used in citing to official state reporters:

Alabama	*Ala., Ala.App.*
Arizona	*Ariz., Ariz.App.*
Arkansas	*Ark.*
California	*Cal., Cal.2d, Cal.3d, Cal.App., Cal.App.2d, Cal.App.3d.*
Colorado	*Colo.*
Connecticut	*Conn.*
Delaware	*Del.*
Georgia	*Ga., Ga.App.*
Hawaii	*Haw.*
Idaho	*Idaho*
Illinois	*Ill., Ill.2d, Ill.App., Ill.App.2d, Ill.App.3d.*
Indiana	*Ind., Ind.App.*
Iowa	*Iowa*
Kansas	*Kan.*
Kentucky	*Ky.*
Louisiana	*La.*
Maine	*Me.*
Maryland	*Md., Md.App.*
Massachusetts	*Mass., Mass.App.Ct.*
Michigan	*Mich., Mich.App.*
Minnesota	*Minn.*
Montana	*Mont.*
Nebraska	*Neb.*
Nevada	*Nev.*
New Hampshire	*N.H.*
New Jersey	*N.J., N.J.Super.*
New Mexico	*N.M.*
New York	*N.Y., N.Y.2d, App.Div., App.Div.2d, Misc., Misc.2d.*

North Carolina	*N.C., N.C.App.*
Ohio	*Ohio St., Ohio St.2d, Ohio App., Ohio App.2d.*
Oregon	*Or., Or.App.*
Pennsylvania	*Pa., Pa.Super.Ct., Pa.Commw.Ct.*
Rhode Island	*R.I.*
South Carolina	*S.C.*
South Dakota	*S.D.*
Tennessee	*Tenn., Tenn.App.*
Utah	*Utah, Utah 2d.*
Vermont	*Vt.*
Virginia	*Va.*
Washington	*Wash., Wash.2d, Wash.App.*
West Virginia	*W.Va.*
Wisconsin	*Wis.*

The following is a list of the most commonly cited unofficial reporters, all of which are part of the West National Reporter System.

Atlantic Reporter	*A.; A.2d*
Connecticut, Delaware, Maine, Maryland, New Hampshire, New Jersey, Pennsylvania, Rhode Island, Vermont	
California Reporter	*Cal.Rptr.*
New York Supplement	*N.Y.S.; N.Y.S.2d*
Northeastern Reporter	*N.E.; N.E.2d*
Illinois, Indiana, Massachusetts, New York, Ohio	
Northwestern Reporter	*N.W.; N.W.2d*
Iowa, Michigan, Minnesota, Nebraska, North Dakota, South Dakota, Wisconsin	
Pacific Reporter	*P.; P.2d*
Alaska, Arizona, California, Colorado, Hawaii, Idaho, Kansas, Montana, Nevada, New Mexico, Oklahoma, Oregon, Utah, Washington, Wyoming	
Southern Reporter	*So.; So.2d*
Alabama, Florida, Louisiana, Mississippi	
Southeastern Reporter	*S.E.; S.E.2d*
Georgia, North Carolina, South Carolina, Virginia, West Virginia	
Southwestern Reporter	*S.W.; S.W.2d*
Arkansas, Kentucky, Missouri, Tennessee, Texas	

III. INDICATING PURPOSE AND WEIGHT

Properly citing an authority includes indicating why the particular authority was cited and its relationship to the proposition advanced. This is done by using introductory signals. The precedential value of a case or statute will also be indicated by the citation. The citation may be supplemented by parentheticals identifying the relationship of the language cited in the brief to the case cited as its source (*e.g.,* holding, dictum, or concurring opinion) or other explanatory statements, as well.

A. SIGNALS INDICATING SUPPORT

Some authority should be cited as the source of each point of law or proposition asserted in an advocate's argument. The relationship between the cited authority and the proposition, or the degree to which the authorities cited support the proposition, are indicated using the following signals. The advocate must decide the purpose for which an authority is being cited and the appropriate signal to indicate this purpose.

1. *[No Signal]*

No introductory signal is used when the proposition asserted in the brief is directly quoted or paraphrased from the cited authority. The absence of a signal also indicates that the proposition is the authority's direct holding. This should be the most common signal used in a brief:

> Some courts have stated that any association, ''however loose or informal,'' which ''furnishes a vehicle for the commission of two or more predicate crimes'' may constitute a RICO enterprise. <u>United States v. Elliott</u>, 571 F.2d 880, 898 (5th Cir.1978).

2. *"E.g."*

"Use *"e.g."* when the cited authority is merely a sampling of a pool of authorities supporting the same proposition. This signal indicates that there are additional cases directly supporting the proposition but citation to them would not be helpful. Combining *"e.g.,"* with other signals will indicate somewhat different relationships. *"See, e.g.,"* indicates that the proposition asserted will be suggested by examining the authority cited, which is only part of a pool of similar authorities. However, *"but see, e.g.,"* indicates that the authority cited is part of a pool of authorities casting doubt upon the proposition discussed.

The signal *"e.g.,"* should always be followed by a comma. Additionally, when used in combination with other signals, *"e.g.,"* should also be preceded by a comma:

Lower courts have spoken of ''the 'economic reality' test'' and have gone on to list only the three prongs of the Howey test for an investment contract, or to refer only to the second half of the Forman analysis as though Forman does not urge an ''economic reality'' analysis in all situations, with non-traditional and conventional instruments. See, e.g., Frederiksen v. Poloway, 637 F.2d 1147 (7th Cir.), cert. denied, 451 U.S. 1017 (1981).

3. "Accord"

An "accord," citation is used to introduce a string of authorities which are in agreement with the authority cited as the direct source of a proposition. This citation is often used when the jurisdiction in which the case is on appeal has very little case law interpretation of the relevant statute. Use "accord" to demonstrate unanimity among various jurisdictions on a single point of law:

Moreover, the reasoning of the district court, on which the lower courts rely, was soundly criticized by the appellate court. The second circuit, citing legislative history, expressly noted that ''[t]he language of the statute . . . does not premise a RICO violation on proof or allegations of any connection with organized crime.'' Moss v. Morgan Stanley, 553 F.Supp. 1347 (S.D.N.Y.), aff'd 719 F.2d 5, 7 (2d Cir.1983); accord, United States v. Forsythe, 560 F.2d 1127, 1136 (3d Cir.1977) (bribery of judges); Owl Construction Co. v. Ronald Adams Contractor, Inc., No. 83-3424, slip op. (5th Cir. March 23, 1984) USACO Coal Co. v. Carbomin Energy, Inc., 689 F.2d 94 (6th Cir.1982) Sutliff, Inc. v. Donovan Companies, No. 83-1308, 83-1499, slip op. (7th Cir. Feb. 9, 1984).

4. "See"

The signal "see" indicates that the authorities which follow the signal constitute the basic source material which supports the asserted proposition. "See" is used instead of "[no signal]" when the proposition is not specifically set out by the cited authority, but follows logically from it. This is also the difference between using "accord" and "see *also* ". Notice that *"see"* is not followed by a comma unless used in combination with *"e.g."*:

> Unlike the passive investor who must rely on others for critical information, the majority purchaser is in a much better position to safeguard his investment and does not need further protections afforded by the securities laws. See Hirsch v. DuPont, 396 F.Supp. 1214 (S.D.N.Y.1975), aff'd. 553 F.2d 750 (2d Cir.1977).

5. *"Cf."*

The weight signal *"cf."* is used when the cited authority supports a proposition different from that asserted but sufficiently analogous to lend support. Literally, *"cf."* means compare. *"Cf."* should not be used without a parenthetical explaining the analogy:

> Since Vitas made ''essential managerial decisions'' affecting the conduct and profitability of Wholesale Computer, namely, the selection and termination of key executive personnel, he cannot be said to have ''relied'' on others within the meaning of a ''securities investment.'' Frederiksen v. Poloway, 637 F.2d 1147, 1150-52 (7th Cir. 1981), cert. denied, 451 U.S. 1017 (1981); cf. Landreth Timber Co. v. Landreth, No. 81-3446, slip op. at 1313 (agreement by seller of a business to serve as consultant to buyer following sale did not affect buyer's control over business, as ''even these services were terminable at the will of the [buyer]'').

In this example, *"cf."* was used because the authority following that signal was not cited as supporting the proposition stated in quotations, but for the comparative value of its factual circumstances. However, it is the use which the advocate makes of a particular authority that determines which signal should be used. Therefore, this same authority may later be cited as the direct source for a statement very similar to the one mentioned.

B. SIGNALS WHICH SUGGEST A PROFITABLE COMPARISON

When comparing one authority to another will suggest or illustrate the statement asserted, the comparison is indicated as follows: *Compare . . . [and] . . . with . . . [and]*. The advocate guides the court to the differences between two different lines of authority, instead of distinguishing the cases in the brief's text, since the authorities which are distinguished may have some general bearing on the case but are not central to the issue on appeal. This method differs from *"cf."* because *"cf."* invites comparisons between the cited authority and the textual statement:

> Even though the Board has often recognized that it had statutory jurisdiction, it was not until the more recent cases that the Board was able to assert jurisdiction. Compare Bodle, Fogel, Julber, Reinhardt and Rothschild, 206 N.L.R.B. 512 (1973) with Evans and Kunz, Ltd., 194 N.L.R.B. 180, Lab. L. Rep. (CCH) ¶18,116 (1977).

C. SIGNALS INDICATING A CONTRARY POSITION

An advocate has a duty to inform the court of authority which is directly adverse and controlling. A contrary signal may be useful as a transition from discussing adverse authority to the main theme of the advocate's case. When introducing contrary authority, the signal indicating this purpose should start a new sentence. It should not be used in the same sentence as signals introducing authorities which support the textual proposition.

1. *"Contra"*

The signal *"Contra,"* is used when the authority cited directly supports the proposition contrary to that in the immediately preceding discussion, just as *"[no signal]"* is used to indicate supporting authority. *"Contra "* is therefore used to introduce a case which the advocate feels must be distinguished while avoiding an unnecessary discussion of such an adverse authority:

> The decision to reorganize a partnership is based on considerations which are particularly suitable for discussion at the bargaining table. See Fibreboard Paper Products Corp. v. NLRB, 379 U.S. 203 (1964). Contra, NLRB v. Thompson Transport Co., 406 F.2d 698 (10th Cir.1969) (where the employer's decision to close was caused by economic factors beyond the control of the parties and for which collective bargaining could have no solution).

2. "But see" and "but cf."

The difference between *"but see"* and *"but cf."* is often just the emphasis the advocate wants to place on the authority cited. When the authority cited would suggest a conclusion contrary to that set forth, use *"but see"*. The term *"but see"* is the counterpart of *"see"*. It is used to introduce authority which inferentially rejects the statement in the text:

> A number of circuit courts have considered the applicability of the federal securities laws to transactions which involve ''stock'' in the traditional sense but which result in the transfer of the business itself from the seller to the purchaser. Courts which have deemed the federal securities laws applicable in these situations have held that if the instruments transferred are ''stock'' within the ordinary meaning of the term, the transaction is, by definition, within the scope of the laws and no further analysis is necessary. See Golden v. Garafalo, 678 F.2d at 1144; Coffin v. Polishing Machines, Inc., 596 F.2d at 1204; Daily v. Morgan, 701 F.2d at 496. But see Frederiksen v. Poloway, 637 F.2d 1147 (7th Cir.1981); Chandler v. Kew, Inc., 691 F.2d 443 (10th Cir.1977); King v. Winkler, 673 F.2d 342 (11th Cir.1982).

When the authority cited supports a proposition analogous to a proposition contrary to that set forth in the text, use *"but cf."* This signal should always be used with an explanatory parenthetical. When either one of these signals follows a similarly contrary signal and authority, the *"but"* is dropped from the signal introducing the subsequent authority.

D. SIGNALS INDICATING BACKGROUND MATERIAL: "SEE GENERALLY" AND "SEE ALSO"

Neither *"See generally"* nor *"See also"* is followed by a comma. Both of these signals should only be used to begin a new citation sentence, not as a part of a citation sentence or phrase which also contains either supporting or contrary authority.

Since the brief is used as a persuasive tool, citation to background information should be limited. The advocate should inform the court by using supporting authority which directly relates to the proposition asserted, or distinguishing authority which deals directly with the relevant cases. General background signals are most often used to introduce secondary authorities.

The signal *"See generally"* is used when the authority cited does not provide support for the specific proposition stated, but provides the reader with a source for obtaining general background on the subject matter discussed in the immediately preceding text. Authorities introduced in this manner are merely informative. *"See generally"* should not be used when a more affirmative signal such as *"see"* would also be appropriate:

> The legislative history behind the inclusion of ''fraud in the sale of securities'' as a RICO predicate act indicates that such a sweeping interpretation is unwarranted. During 1969, Congress became aware of a growing problem of theft and fraudulent resale of securities when the president of the New York Stock Exchange testified before a House subcommittee about the problem of securities thefts. See generally, Securities Market Agencies: Hearings on the Administration of the Laws Pertaining to the Regulation of the Securities Markets by the Administrative Agency and by the Self-Regulatory Agencies Involved Before the Subcomm. on Commerce and Finance of the House Comm. on Interstate and Foreign Commerce, 91st Cong., 1st Sess. 137 (1969).

The signal *"See also"* is used when the authority cited provides background to a question on an analogous proposition and also provides a comparison to the stated proposition would provide additional background perspective. This signal differs from *"cf."* and *"but see"* since it is not cited as supporting or contrasting authority. Rather, it is used to introduce an authority which provides background information as a point which is analogous to the proposition:

> Heeding Senator McClellan's words, the ''greater number'' of courts which have reviewed RICO have reiterated that a competitive injury is not necessary. Schacht v. Brown, 711 F.2d 1343 (7th Cir.) cert. denied, ___ U.S. ___, 52 U.S.L.W. 3423 (Nov. 28, 1983). See also Bennett v. Berg, 685 F.2d 1053, 1059, aff'd en banc, 710 F.2d 1361 (8th Cir.1983) (''[A]lthough RICO borrowed the tools of antitrust law to combat organized criminal ac-

```
tivity, we do not believe the RICO Act was
limited to the antitrust goal of preventing
interference with free trade.'')
```

Remember, if an authority is introduced by the signal *"See also "* for one citation, it does not necessarily mean that the same weight signal must be used in any other citation to that authority. In this example the same authority previously introduced by *"see also "* is cited as the basic source of the statement in the text.

Thus, a signal is used more to describe the advocate's use of the authority than the information contained in that authority. The signal should be used to guide the court to those sources which the advocate wants the court to review. The more the advocate wants the court to review its authorities, the more direct the signal should be. Generally, direct citations will include the page which the advocate wants the court to examine, whereas general background citations will usually be to the authority as a whole.

E. ORDER OF PRESENTING SIGNALS

Authorities should be presented in the most persuasive order if more than one authority is cited in connection with a single proposition. One way this is accomplished is by placing the most direct signals first. The other is by placing the authorities following each introductory signal into reverse chronological order, giving priority to decisions rendered by the higher courts.

When more than one signal is used in connection with a single statement, the signals (together with the authorities they introduce) should appear in the order in which they were presented in the preceding material:

1) [no signal];

2) *e.g.,*;

3) *accord,,*;

4) *see* (*see e.g.,*);

5) *cf.*;

6) *Compare . . . with . . .*;

7) *Contra,,*;

8) *but see,,*;

10) *See generally;*

11) *see also,*

A signal should only appear once in connection with any one statement. That is, every authority cited as being in *"accord"* should appear with every other authority bearing the same weight and relationship to the statement.

The authorities cited following a single signal are given in this order: cases, statutes, and secondary authority. This order places the most persuasive authorities first. Case authority should appear before statutory authorities because the cases are usually interpretations of the more general statutes. This, however, is only the general rule. Should a particular proposition call for a different order as being more persuasive, that order should be used. Consistency itself can help maintain a persuasive flow, variation from the general rule should be avoided unless the variation naturally follows. Within each subgroup of cases, statutes, or secondary authority, there are also general rules prescribing the order of the citations.

1. Case Law

Decisions emanating from a higher court in the same jurisdiction are more persuasive. In arranging the cases by their respective courts of decision, all United States courts of appeal are treated as one court. Nevertheless, the advocate may differentiate among the circuit court opinions by placing cases decided within the circuit hearing the appeal first. Furthermore, when an appeal is taken within the state system, the most persuasive order of presentation may not be the same as if the case were before a federal court.

Cases decided by the same court are listed in reverse chronological order (the most recent decisions first). In a federal appeal, cases cited in connection with a single weight signal should appear in the following order:

Federal Sources:

    (1) United States Supreme Court decisions;

    (2) United States courts of appeal;

    (3) District courts;

    (4) Administrative agencies (in alphabetical order);

State Sources:

    (5) state court decisions (in alphabetical order by state, then by rank of the court within each state);

    (6) state agencies (in alphabetical order by state, then alphabetically within each state).

This is not to recommend that citations should be strung together. No more authorities should be cited than are absolutely necessary to support the advocate's point. Citing too many cases interrupts the flow of an argument. It is better to analyze thoroughly a few closely related cases than to waste space on needless citation.

2. *Statutes*

Just as with cases, the strongest and most applicable statutes should be cited first following each signal. Next, statutes generally applicable to the proposition should be listed, usually following background signals. The order in which statutory authorities should generally appear is as follows:

a. Constitutions (United States Constitution first and then state constitutions in alphabetical order by state).

b. Federal statutes:

—currently in force and in U.S.C. or U.S.C.A. (by progressive order of U.S.C. title number);

—currently in force but not in U.S.C. or U.S.C.A. (most recently adopted first and thereafter in reverse chronological order);

—repealed (by order of date of repeal, the most recently repeated first and thereafter in reverse chronological order).

c. Rules, regulations, and administrative materials should follow the pattern generally applicable in statutes.

3. *Secondary Materials*

Within each of the following categories, citations are listed in reverse chronological order, and within any one time period by alphabetical order according to the author's last name or, if the author is unknown, by title. Secondary material should be presented in the following order:

a. Legislative history;

b. Treatises (by date of the particular volume or supplement);

c. Books;

d. Articles;

e. Student-written law review material (list alphabetically by the name of the periodical);

f. Informal materials such as lectures or seminars (Because the court may not have access to such information, the pertinent parts should be attached to the appendix with a description of the nature of the presentation and the organization or individual making the presentation).

This is a general ordering based on the weight the court may give to an authority within any one of these categories. This order should be changed if a particular secondary authority would be more persuasive than another.

F. CITATION PARENTHETICALS

Parentheticals may be used following a citation to provide the reader with additional facts explaining why the particular authority was cited. Like introductory signals, parentheticals used for different purposes are separated. It is possible to have more than one parenthetical following a citation. In such a case, the parentheticals should be presented in the following order:

(1) Parentheticals indicating weight;

(2) Explanatory parentheticals;

(3) Informative parentheticals

Each of these parentheticals is described below.

1. *Parentheticals Indicating Weight*

Parenthetical comment is another tool which can be used to indicate the persuasiveness of the authorities cited. When the statement in the text represents something other than the majority holding of a case cited in connection with that statement, this must be indicated in parentheses immediately following the citation. Among the most common forms indicating weight are:

(1) "(dictum)"

(2) "(concurring opinion)"

(3) "(dissenting opinion)"

(4) [points decided by implication] "(by implication)" or "(alternative holding)"

(5) [points on which the holding of the court is not clear] "(semble)".

For example, if the advocate wanted to cite the concurring opinion in *Fibreboard Paper Products Corp. v. NLRB*, 379 U.S. 203 (1964), as providing the basic source material for a statement in the text, the citation might appear as follows:

```
See Fibreboard Paper Products Corp. v. NLRB,
379 U.S. 203, 217 (1964) (concurring opin-
ion).
```

In this example, "*see*" ties the statement in the text to this case as a basic source for this line of reasoning. The parenthetical is necessary, however, to show that the basic source material supporting the statement is in the concurring rather than the majority opinion.

2. *Explanatory Parentheticals*

Explanatory parentheticals are used to provide certain additional information about the opinion. For example: "([Judge's name])" "(4–3 decision)" "(per curiam)" "(memorandum opinion)". Thus, the information contained in a parenthetical indicating weight may also serve as the basis for an explanatory parentheticals at another point in the brief. Because explanatory parentheticals provide additional information to supplement the authority cited or the preceding parenthetical, there is no limit to the number of parentheticals that may be used following a single citation:

> See Fibreboard Paper Products Corp. v. NLRB, supra (concurring opinion) (Stewart, J.) (Douglas and Harlan, JJ., joining) (5-Justice Majority) (Goldberg, J., took no part).

Whenever this many parentheticals are necessary, the case should be discussed more fully in the text.

3. *Informative Parentheticals*

This category of parenthetical is used to provide the reader with a short statement about the case, or to include a comment on the case which helps explain the citation. The informative parenthetical follows the parenthetical indicating weight and the explanatory parenthetical, but the informative parenthetical may also be used without the other forms of parentheticals. There should only be one informative parenthetical per citation. If further description is required, perhaps the case should be more fully discussed in the text.

> Mr. Steak v. River City Steak, Inc., 460 F.2d 666 (10th Cir.1972) (mere delegation of authority over daily operations held not to affect franchisee's control over his business).

G. RELATED AUTHORITY

Phrases identifying related authorities are also appended in a citation to provide the reader with further information about the case or statute cited in the text. These other authorities are related to the cited authority in such a manner as to refer the reader to another work which (1) conveniently reprints the cited authority, (2) provides the prior or subsequent history of a case, (3) discusses or quotes the cited authority, or (4) is quoted or discussed in the cited authority.

References to related authority are generally introduced by an underscored explanatory phrase which follows the citation and immediately precedes the related authority. The explanatory phrase describes the relationship between the cited authority and the related authority:

> Frankfurter, Some Reflections on the Reading of Statutes, 47 Colum.L.Rev. 527, 533 (1947); Quoted in Blakey, The RICO Civil Fraud Action

> in Context: Reflections on Bennet v. Berg, 58
> Notre Dame L.Rev. 237, 285, n. 145 (1982).

Note, no comma follows the explanatory phrase in the above example. When introducing the subsequent history of a case a comma will usually follow the explanatory phrase:

> Frederiksen v. Poloway, 637 F.2d 1147 (7th
> Cir.), cert. denied, 451 U.S. 1017 (1981).

If more than one type of related authority is used, these additional authorities should be presented in the following order: reprinted authorities, relevant history, authorities discussing the cited authority, and authorities discussed by the cited authority.

In only one instance should the explanatory phrase not be underlined. Where the related authority is discussed or quoted in the cited authority, the relationship between the two authorities is explained in a parenthetical:

> Frankfurter, Some Reflections on the Reading
> of Statutes, 47 Colum.L.Rev. 527, 533 (1947),
> cited in Blakey, The RICO Civil Fraud Action
> in Context: Reflections on Bennet v. Berg, 58
> Notre Dame L.Rev. 237, 285, n. 145 (1982) (applying Justice Frankfurter's ideas to 18
> U.S.C. § 1961).

Other common explanatory phrases which describe the relationship between authorities are: *"noted in"*, *"quoted in"*, *"reviewed by"*, *"questioned in"*, *"(noting)"*, *"(quoting)"*, *"cert. granted"*, *"vacated"*, *"appeal denied"*, *"enforcement denied"*, and *"modified"*.

Chapter Four

THE ORAL ARGUMENT

Oral argument is the advocate's final chance to convince the court of the client's position. In oral argument, the advocate is able to answer the court's questions and address its concerns. When the advocate determines that oral argument may advance a client's interests and when the court agrees to hear oral argument, the advocate must be well prepared.

There is a distinction between the Moot Court situation and an actual appellate hearing. Moot Court is designed to evaluate the ability of the advocate, while an appellate hearing is an adjudication of the merits of the case. It does not necessarily follow, however, that the two situations should be approached differently. Although the attention of the tribunal is on the one hand drawn to the individual advocate, and on the other to the client's position, excellence in both situations will ensue from precisely the same techniques. These techniques include preparation, organization, good speaking skills and an awareness of the court's concerns.

I. DESCRIPTION OF A HEARING

It is first necessary to understand what actually occurs during the appellate hearing to understand how to prepare and present an oral argument. For descriptive purposes, the hearing will be broken down into the general procedure and the specific elements of a presentation.

A. GENERAL PROCEDURE

The hearing is usually conducted before a three-judge tribunal. The advocate faces the bench from behind a lectern or podium. The petitioner is entitled to make the first presentation and may also reserve time for rebuttal. After counsel for petitioner has spoken, but before he delivers a rebuttal, counsel for the responding party is offered the opportunity to address the court. During these presentations, the court will frequently interject comments or queries, requesting the advocate to address its specific concerns. Following these arguments, the court indicates it will take the matter under submission or recesses to reach a decision.

Regulations governing procedural aspects of the appellate hearing may be found in the local court rules. The Moot Court Rules at the University of California at Los Angeles, for example, require that each party be represented by two advocates, each of whom is permitted to speak for up to fifteen minutes. The advocate presenting the rebuttal may reserve up to three minutes of time for rebuttal, but this must be done at the beginning of the advocate's initial speech.

B. ELEMENTS OF A PRESENTATION

The oral argument contains an introduction, prepared argument, answer to questions from the tribunal, transitions back to the argument, summary of uncovered materials, and conclusion. While all of these elements might not occur in a single presentation, it is important that the advocate be familiar with their purpose and use.

An introduction is an opening statement to the court which informs the court of purely formal matters, such as identifying the advocate and the client, delineating the issues to be discussed by the advocate, and reserving rebuttal time. Since the court will be familiar with the general fact pattern of the case from the briefs, further information need not be provided in the introduction. Rather, the introductory portion should capsulize the central idea the advocate wishes the court to keep in mind.

After the introduction, the advocate begins to present the argument to the court. This is normally a prepared argument of two parts: a summary of the main contentions and an argument of individual points. In summarizing the contentions, the advocate should enumerate the various arguments and subpoints which make the contentions compelling. After the enumeration, the most important and persuasive subpoints are asserted.

At various points throughout the argument, the advocate will be interrupted by questions from the bench. The advocate must answer these questions in the most responsive, complete, and persuasive way possible. After responding, the advocate must return to the prepared argument by using an appropriate transition sentence.

II. OUTLINING THE ARGUMENT

The first step in preparing a presentation is to construct an outline. An outline should be prepared even if the advocate plans on using different notes, or no notes, during the hearing. Mere preparation of the outline will help the advocate to understand the substance, supporting materials, and organization of the argument.

A. PURPOSES OF THE OUTLINE

The outline serves three purposes: it provides a conceptual framework for the argument and its supporting materials; it organizes the materials from which an extemporaneous speech can be delivered; and, it enables the advocate to handle questions from the bench.

First, the outline structures the materials for the advocate and, ultimately, for the court. By articulating at the outset of the argument the contentions listed in the outline, the advocate provides the court with an idea of the critical elements to be discussed.

Second, the proposed outline guides the advocate in presenting the argument. By following the outline and discussing the points of analysis supporting the advocate's contentions, the advocate presents an oral argument which is both persuasive and logical. Note that the argument of individual points is presented through the use of facts in conjunction with legal precedents and public policy. These most specific elements of the outline help the advocate demonstrate why the client should prevail.

Third, the outline aids the advocate in responding to questions posed by the court. Since the outline will be an organized analysis of all the major issues in the case, with references to legal authority, case facts, and equitable policy considerations, the advocate need merely look to the outline to find the subject of the court's question, respond to the query and continue arguing the contentions.

B. BUILDING THE OUTLINE

Building a skeletal outline of the argument is a relatively simple process. The advocate should list the contentions, points of analysis which support those contentions, and the factual or legal authority used as the basis for such analysis in the brief. In addition, the advocate should include unfavorable legal authorities and ways in which they can be distinguished from the case on appeal. In most cases, the outline prepared for the hearing will closely resemble the outline of the brief.

In preparing the outline, the advocate must attempt to determine what the court will view as the legal issues crucial to a decision in the case. These issues should then be treated in greater detail in the outline. While the level of specificity in the outline will vary with each advocate, it is recommended that this outline be no longer than one or two pages so that it can be used for quick reference at the hearing. For example, the petitioner in *Vitas v. Younger & Burton* may outline the RICO argument as follows:

<u>THE DISTRICT COURT ERRED IN DISMISSING ROCKY VITAS' RICO CLAIM.</u>

A. Congress intended RICO to be a broad-based remedy.

<u>TURKETTE</u>: Language of statute conclusive. Sen. McClellan: RICO applies to all persons.

<u>SCHACT, MOSS, CAMPANELE</u>: All federal courts refuse to apply an ''organized crime'' requirement.

B. Vitas has alleged a RICO ''enterprise.''

<u>TURKETTE</u>: Group of individuals associated in fact. Proof of enterprise and of racketeering activity may coalesce.

C. Vitas has alleged a RICO injury.

<u>STATUTORY LANGUAGE</u>: ''Any person injured in his business or property by reason of a (RICO) violation may sue therefor . . . and shall recover threefold the damages he sustains and the cost of his suit.''

<u>RUSSELO</u>: Must be construed broadly to attack racketeering at its economic roots.

III. PRESENTING THE ORAL ARGUMENT

To prepare effectively for the various contingencies in the oral hearing, the advocate should first prepare the outline. The outline should then be reviewed carefully to anticipate possible questions and to formulate responses. The final step is to prepare an introduction and conclusion to the oral argument.

A. INTRODUCTION

The introduction should set the tone of the argument. The advocate must capitalize on the court's initial attention by couching both the facts and issues in an accurate but persuasive manner. This can be done using a thesis statement expressing the central idea which the advocate wants the court to remember throughout the argument. The thesis is a one-sentence affirmative capsulization of the most persuasive theme in the advocate's argument. The thesis may be based on the policy considerations, case law, or the equities in the case. Although the thesis statement should be composed in advance, the advocate should be sensitive to the court's concerns and should be prepared to modify the thesis accordingly:

> A: Your Honors. My name is Susan Keller. I am
> counsel for the petitioner, Rocky Vitas.
> This afternoon I will explain how the
> shares of stock in Wholesale Computer
> which Mr. Vitas purchased are securities,
> thus qualifying him for the special pro-
> tections of the anti-fraud provisions of
> the Securities Acts. Mr. Vitas was induced
> by the misrepresentations and deceptions
> of respondents Younger and Burton to in-
> vest his savings in shares of stock in
> Wholesale Computer. This enterprise was
> represented to him as being ''highly prof-
> itable and successful.'' On the contrary,
> the company is losing great sums of money
> and his investment is diminishing rapidly
> in value. These same respondents, through
> their Motion to Dismiss, would now deny Mr.
> Vitas an opportunity to have his claim
> heard in federal court.

This introduction not only provides the court with essential factual information within the context of the issues involved, but it does so in a way which is designed to evoke a favorable response to the advocate's position—it is clearly part of her argument. Note that, the advocate may wish to use the more formal salutation, "May it please the Court," instead of "Your Honors."

B. PREPARED ARGUMENT

After the introduction, the advocate presents the substance of the argument. This argument is drawn from the contentions and analysis prepared in the outline.

1. Selection of Arguments

It is not necessary that the advocate orally argue every point listed in the outline; in fact, it is generally a mistake to repeat all of the arguments of the brief. Unnecessarily repeating arguments presented in the brief will bore the court and waste its time. An argument is not waived merely because it is not developed in oral argument. The advocate should select only the most crucial arguments for oral presentation and should include all arguments needed to win. Evasion of vital weaknesses is never persuasive. On the other hand, the advocate should avoid subjecting weak arguments to the bench's scrutiny, if possible.

In selecting the arguments to be presented, the advocate should keep in mind a few basic rules. Selecting arguments is at least somewhat dependent upon the side being represented. For example, the advocate representing the appellant or petitioner should select arguments which show that reversible error was committed by the lower court. Counsel for respondent or appellee, on the other hand, should select arguments which show that the trial court either applied the correct legal standard or properly exercised its discretion. The order in which the advocates present their respective cases has a bearing on the selection of arguments. The advocate who argues first has the disadvantage of not really knowing what issues the court perceives to be crucial to a determination of the case. The advocate must therefore rely on a predetermined sense of the case, trends in the law, and knowledge of the court and its members in selecting the arguments to be presented. The advocate arguing second, on the other hand, can discern the court's concerns by listening to the court's questions, and modifying the arguments accordingly. Above all, all advocates must know their legal and factual arguments, and must be flexible enough to add or delete arguments to meet the court's concerns.

The advocate should concentrate on two or three arguments rather than restating all the arguments in the brief. If, in preparing for oral argument, the advocate discovers that some helpful point was not sufficiently emphasized in the brief, oral argument may be used to provide that emphasis.

Techniques of oral presentation are not ends in themselves; the goal of oral argument is to persuade the court. The advocate should not insist on pursuing a line of reasoning which is unacceptable to the court when other arguments are available. There may be many reasons why a court does not want to base its decision on certain grounds, and the advocate must be perceptive enough to discover the road of least resistance leading to the desired result. However, flexibility does not imply surrender. When an argument is crucial to the case, it should be made with vigor and tenacity regardless of the court's predisposition against it. The effective advocate readily discerns the times to follow the court and the times to lead it.

2. Using Authority

When orally arguing contentions, the advocate should be wary of citing too many cases to the court. Most briefs substantiate all points that are made with ample case authority. This technique does not work well in the oral presentation. The court will not be able to follow or remember too many cases. Consequently, authority must be selected with care. The advocate should present only those cases most directly on point, relating to the most important arguments.

Although it is usually safe to assume that the judges have read the brief, counsel cannot assume that they remember the facts of all the cases cited. Without a factual context, most cases are useless as authority. Thus, whenever the court's attention is drawn to a case, a full discussion of the facts should be given as well as a discussion of the legal doctrine.

The "rule" given above is not to be followed universally. Occasions arise where the case cited does not need factual elaboration. If the case is particularly well-known or was recently decided by the same court, reference by name is appropriate.

If the case is cited in the brief, it is usually sufficient in oral argument to identify the case by name, jurisdiction, and date alone. If, on the other hand, the case is not cited in the brief, the court should be informed of this and provided with a full citation to the case. The advocate must not assume, however, that the court shares his detailed familiarity with the case.

Statutes and decisions should be quoted only when the language significantly adds to the clarity or persuasiveness of the oral argument. Hearing is a poor mechanism for catching verbal refinements, so quotations should generally be limited to presentation in a brief. The advocate should not attempt to direct the court in the precise arrangement of words or the phrasing of a quotation. Rather, the court should be directed to the underlying meaning of the material by paraphrasing the quotation.

There are times, however, when quotation is necessary. These occasions arise with particular frequency when statutory construction or definitional meaning is involved. In these cases, the precise language may determine the disposition of the case. An effective method of assisting the court in these instances is to invite the court's attention to the particular page of the brief on which the quotation appears. This permits the court to follow the words and, by combining both visual and aural perception, to grasp the significance of the quoted language.

There is a serious drawback, however, in citing to the brief—a disadvantage common to most visual aids. Whenever such aids are employed, the bench can become so involved that some or all judges may stop listening momentarily as their minds linger upon what they are seeing. It is imperative that the court follow the presentation of the advocate at the pace which the advocate is setting; the advocate should be extremely selective in choosing only the most vital language to lay before the court.

If a statute is important enough to form the body of an argument on oral presentation, it is important enough to be set forth in the brief. Thus, there should be no problem in simply calling the court's attention to the relevant pages of the brief while making a statutory argument. Since the advocate's primary objective is to communicate, devices should be selected which will assist in the presentation. These observations lead not only to the conclusion that the advocate should cite to the brief, but also that arguments on statutory construction should be kept as simple as possible.

3. Repeating Arguments

The advocate should not hesitate to repeat main contentions throughout the argument. Obviously the advocate should not sound like a broken record; the reiteration of contentions should be made within the context of the responses to questions, the transitions from one issue to another, and the conclusions.

The need for repetition is greatest when the court is actively questioning the advocate. Often some members of the panel are thinking about their next question while the advocate is answering a question from someone else. It is the advocate's obligation to make sure that all of the judges have understood the main points. It would be a rare case indeed, where one simple statement and argument could accomplish this goal.

4. Handling Opponent's Arguments

In the oral argument the advocate must answer the relevant contentions advanced by opposing counsel. These answers can be effectively presented within the framework of the outline. The advocate should not debate specific legal principles with opposing counsel. Instead, he should couch his responses within the analysis of his own contentions as an affirmative posture is more persuasive than a point-by-point refutation of contentions raised by the opposition.

C. RESPONDING TO QUESTIONS

Many appeals are determined by how well the advocate responds to questions from the bench. Questions not only evince an interest in the ongoing oral presentation, but also reveal the court's thoughts and concerns. Accordingly, questions should be welcomed by the advocate and answered with care.

The advocate should not evade or postpone a question no matter how embarrassing the question may be or how much it interrupts the argument's organization. The court has the right to expect and receive prompt replies to its questions. A well-prepared advocate who has a sound position should have no trouble responding to the court. Although the tribunal's questions may interrupt the logical order of the advocate's outline, the court's questions should never be deferred to a later time in the argument. To delay responding only increases the court's apprehension, and leaves the impression that the advocate cannot effectively respond to the court's questions.

The advocate should expect that the court will interrupt the structured argument, and should design the outline so that an immediate shift can be executed smoothly. Many arguments, in fact, are composed almost entirely of questions from the bench and the advocates' responses. Consequently, the advocate must be prepared to answer questions and should also have a brief summation of the main point in case the court only allows two to three minutes to summarize a case after rigorous questioning.

1. Types of Questions

While the court may question the advocate on any subject relevant to the case, questions will usually fall within three main areas: legal authorities, policy considerations, and factual information.

a. Authority

Questions concerning the legal authorities which affect the advocate's contentions require an ability to interpret and distinguish statutes and prior court opinions. The court may want to know how a particular authority supports the advocate's contention, why a conflicting authority supports the advocate's contention, or why a conflicting authority should not govern the court's decision in the case. Sometimes the court merely wishes to discover whether the advocate has any legal authority upon which to base the analysis. To a court bound by principles of *stare decisis,* answers to these questions are very important in persuading the tribunal that it may rule in the advocate's favor.

Judges may also wish to question the advocate concerning the ramifications of principles enunciated by the cited legal authorities. Judges are especially interested in the potential limits of the principles applied by the advocate. In responding to questions regarding the scope and limits of legal principles, the advocate must be prepared to establish the practicable boundaries to which these principles should apply. Judges concerned with extending principles beyond all reasonable limits must be reassured by the advocate that the principle under discussion will not be applied in an overbroad manner:

Q: What would a RICO injury be? Give us a con-
crete example.

A: The language of RICO mandates that there
not be injury merely from predicate acts of
racketeering, but from the involvement of
an enterprise. Section 1962 of the statute
explicitly states that there would have to
be something more than predicate acts. For
example, the infiltration of a business,
or the use of proceeds of racketeering to
run a business are some of the things that
were discussed in Congress. It would seem,
therefore, that if Congress wanted to create a federal RICO remedy for mere acts of
sales fraud, it could have said that anyone
may sue who was injured by reason of acts
of racketeering.

b. *Policy Ramifications and Equitable Considerations*

Questions concerning policy ramifications and equitable considerations require the advocate to look beyond a favorable decision in the
instant case to discern its effect upon the judicial process and society as
a whole. Questions relating to policy considerations involve determining whether the legal principles advanced by the advocate would
promote or hinder desired public policies. These questions are vitally
important to the court because of the impact this particular decision
might have upon society and its institutions. The following example
demonstrates the concern judges have in aligning their decision with
desired public policies, and how an adept advocate can assuage their
concerns:

A: This court may deem that ordinary corporate stock with all of the traditional attributes of the security is to be held in
security. This is the kind of test that an
investor, an unsophisticated investor such
as Mr. Vitas, applies prospectively. He
can see that these things are present, and
it only creates confusion for the investors who purchase the stock that turns out
not to be a security when we have to get into the transactional kind of *Howey* analysis. So we urge this court to uphold its
finding in *United Housing v. Forman* that
the first analysis of the name of the
traditional attributes in the case of or-

dinary performance stock is sufficient and
that only unusual instruments are necessarily subjected to the *Howey* test.

When a judge poses questions regarding the equities of the case,
the advocate should understand that the court is concerned whether
simple justice between the parties requires a particular result. These
questions are important because the court will want to base its decision
not only on case law and policy considerations, but also on broader,
more discretionary principles. The advocate should already have determined which actions by both parties constitute just or unjust conduct,
in order to reassure the court that a decision favoring the advocate's
client is also the just determination of the case:

> Q: What is there so magical about people who
> invest in stocks instead of buying a gro-
> cery store, or a variety of other places
> where they can equally get defrauded?

> A: At the time Congress enacted the legisla-
> tion in 1933 and '34 they were concerned
> with providing a federal remedy for secur-
> ities that could be purchased across state
> lines, that could be purchased on national
> exchanges, and they also extended these
> protections to securities that are ordina-
> ry corporate stock, such as is the case
> here. Indeed, there is a common law fraud
> remedy for the other defrauded purchasers.
> But because Mr. Vitas purchased securi-
> ties, he should be accorded the federal
> remedies that Congress has provided. We
> urge this interpretation upon the court
> because it is mandated by the reading of
> the Securities Acts, the definition of se-
> curities, by the intent of Congress in en-
> acting this remedial legislation, and by
> previous cases which have been decided by
> the court.

c. Information

Finally, the court may question the advocate merely seeking factual information regarding the case on appeal. Answers to these questions typically involve clarifying the court's understanding of the actions which resulted in litigation between the parties or the procedural
posture of the case. The way in which the advocate responds to these
questions is important because the court's decision will be based upon
what it perceives to be the crucial facts involved in the case. The

advocate must be prepared to argue the facts of the case persuasively, as the following example demonstrates:

> Q: Didn't Mr. Vitas retain the power to fire Mr. Burton at any time?
>
> A: Yes, Your Honor. And in fact, Mr. Vitas did fire Mr. Burton only after it became obvious that Wholesale Computer was being run into the ground. However, this was the only time Mr. Vitas was in any way involved with the day-to-day operations of the business, and at all other times relied completely on the efforts of others. As was the case in *Glenn v. Turner Enterprises,* it was the managerial efforts of others which affected the success or failure of Wholesale Computers.

Notice, the advocate answered the request for information, provided additional facts from the record, and cited an authority which helped her case.

2. *Preparing for Questions*

Preparation for the oral argument involves more than merely reviewing the research embodied in the brief. The well-prepared advocate must master the arguments and authorities of his opponent. Preparation is essential if the advocate is to be able to answer questions from the tribunal. To prepare for the court's questions, the advocate should re-read the record on appeal, examining and analyzing every relevant fact of the case so that he will be able to use these facts when responding to queries. The advocate should be familiar with the facts and holding of each case cited in the written brief, as judges often will ask for explanations of how cited authorities support the contentions being advanced.

When preparing for policy oriented questions, the advocate should examine every contention in the outline to determine the legal principle enunciated, and attempt to define its limits. Even when the advocate does not propose a new principle, but merely the application of an established doctrine to a new factual situation, this different application of the principle will raise questions concerning its scope in future cases before the tribunal. Thus, the advocate will want to establish limits to the principle which are reasonable and acceptable to the court. Equitable considerations raised by the facts must also be analyzed. The advocate should prepare for questions regarding the equities in the case by examining the facts and law applicable to each contention, and discovering the most persuasive way to explain their consequences in light of the court's predilections.

Another effective method of preparing for questions from the bench is to work with a partner who can test the advocate's ability to respond to potential questions. The questioner should pursue every conceivable fact, legal principle, policy ramification, and equitable consideration raised by the contentions in the written brief, working with the advocate to create the most persuasive answers possible to these questions. Questions regarding the procedural posture of the case and the remedies requested in the brief should also be considered so that these issues can be handled adroitly if they are raised at the oral hearing.

3. *Effective Responses*

Once the advocate is prepared to respond to questions, the queries posed by the tribunal will aid in presenting the case. These inquiries provide the basis for the advocate's affirmative arguments and reveal the court's approach to the various issues raised by both sides.

By listening carefully to the judges' questions the advocate may discover which judges are persuaded by public policy considerations and which members of the court are concerned with conceptual refinements. This should cue perceptive advocates to modify their arguments accordingly. Furthermore, listening to the questions is important to the advocate's responsiveness. It is not unusual for an advocate to read more into a question than was intended. No question should be answered until it is fully understood, and politely asking the court to repeat a question is less damaging than giving an unsolicited and unresponsive answer.

Not all questions coming from the tribunal are meant to challenge the advocate's position. Sometimes questions are designed to draw out a particular line of reasoning which the court finds especially appealing, or to redirect the advocate's attention to the dispositive issues. Each question should be evaluated before it is answered so that friendly questions are not rejected. The advocate should pause to consider the question asked, if such a pause would be helpful. There is no premium on speedy response, inasmuch as judges are persuaded by the content of responses and not by immediacy or glibness.

Above all the advocate must remain composed. In particular, it is essential that proper deference to the court be shown regardless of the advocate's personal opinion of the question or members of the panel. The advocate must answer every question with a view toward the client's interest and an awareness that an attorney's responses and demeanor affect those interests.

4. *Problematic and Unanswerable Questions*

Notwithstanding the advocate's thorough preparation, the appellate court may often pose questions which the advocate cannot easily answer. Perhaps the appellate court's question is couched in confusing terms or addresses points of law which the advocate failed to consider. Or, the advocate may simply be caught not knowing the precise answer to an obvious and clear question. When faced with these predicaments the advocate has several alternatives.

a. Confusing Questions

When a question is phrased in confusing terms, the advocate should accept responsibility for the confusion and politely ask the judge for clarification:

> Q: What is the meaning of the words ''ascertainable structure?'' Do they ring a bell?
>
> A: I'm sorry, Your Honor. I'm not certain that I understand what you mean. Could you please re-state the question?
>
> Q: The *Bledsoe* decision states that a RICO enterprise must have an ascertainable structure. What did that case hold?

Obviously, such a request for clarification would not be appropriate when it might antagonize the court. For example, the advocate should not request clarification when such a request has previously been made.

b. Irrelevant Questions

When a question delves into points of law which the advocate considers tangential, the advocate should attempt to respond to the court's concern while indicating why that concern—although appealing—is not dispositive of the case.

> Q: Suppose a group of players has a weekly poker game. Two of the players, one day, really want to strike it rich and bring in a marked deck and really skin one of the players. Is there a RICO violation?
>
> A: No, Your Honor, because it does not affect interstate commerce.
>
> Q: One of the players is from out of state.
>
> A: It still wouldn't necessarily affect interstate commerce.
>
> Q: Even if they called him on the telephone?
>
> A: Well, Your Honor, while it may affect interstate commerce, it is a different fact situation than the one before us today. Here, interstate commerce has been affected by a pair of ''decks'' bent on defrauding innocent investors, not gamblers.

Note that in responses of this sort, the advocate must be careful to maintain a deferential attitude.

c. Unanswerable Questions

Clearly the most damaging questions are those which are clear, cogent, pertinent, and a surprise to the advocate. When confronted with this problem, the advocate should seek to minimize the impact of any apparent ignorance. This is occasionally accomplished when the advocate politely and simply acknowledges an inability to answer the question:

> Q: Were all of those cases decided on motions to dismiss?
>
> A: I am sorry, Your Honor, but I am not sure. However, all of these cases were decided by this court, applying the *Howey* test to sales of corporate stock.

An alternative is to offer to provide a supplemental brief on the issue. Of course, this alternative is feasible only if supplemental briefs are allowed by the local court rules.

The advocate may occasionally elicit assistance from the court in responding to troubling questions. For example, if the court asks an advocate to distinguish a case and the advocate cannot remember the precise facts of the case, the advocate might respond in the following way:

> Q: What was the holding in *U.S. v. Errico?*
>
> A: I'm sorry, Your Honor, but I cannot remember the case. Would the court refresh my memory?
>
> Q: Certainly. It was the 1980 horse-fixing case . . .
>
> A: Thank you, Your Honor. In *Errico* a group of individuals conspired to fix horse races at a number of tracks. Despite the changing membership of the group, the Second Circuit found that the group as a whole constituted a RICO enterprise.

The advocate should give an answer that is somewhat non-responsive to the question only as a last resort. This type of dodge should be avoided because it raises questions about the advocate's ethics and credibility.

d. Questions Within Co-counsel's Expertise

An advocate should be familiar with any contentions to be argued by co-counsel. However, if confronted with questions on the co-coun-

sel's issue, the advocate should attempt to give the court some information in response to the question, while politely informing the tribunal
that the question can be answered better by co-counsel:

> A: Your Honor, Ms. Helppie, who will be dis-
> cussing the RICO cause of action, is more
> familiar with this issue than I. However,
> Congress clearly intended RICO to be
> broadly construed in order to meet the
> problem of organized criminals infiltrat-
> ing legitimate businesses. I'm sure my co-
> counsel will be happy to elaborate on this
> in her presentation.

If the Court continues to ask questions on the same issue, each succeeding answer might reveal less and less information and defer more
and more to co-counsel. For example:

> Q: But Congress surely did not intend to in-
> volve the federal courts in ''garden-vari-
> ety'' sales fraud cases?

> A: Briefly, Your Honor. We cannot be sure of
> where the line between ''garden variety''
> cases stops, and where criminals hiding
> behind legitimate businesses begins. My
> co-counsel can elaborate on this in her
> presentation.

Finally, when the advocate cannot answer the question, she or he
should defer entirely to co-counsel:

> Q: But counselor, won't this case necessitate
> federal courts hearing cases involving Mom
> and Pop grocery stores selling overpriced
> goods?

> A: No, Your Honor, it won't. I'll have to de-
> fer to my co-counsel to explain why RICO
> will not extend that far.

Responding to the questions in this manner, the advocate politely but
firmly defers to co-counsel, while nonetheless giving a superficial response.

There are, however, situations in which the advocate will not
follow this type of response pattern. If the advocate is well versed in
co-counsel's arguments, or feels comfortable enough to fully argue
them, the questions can be directly answered without any qualifica-
tions. On the other hand, if the advocate knows something about co-
counsel's arguments but is afraid that the answer might cause problems, deference to co-counsel should be made immediately without

revealing any information. Of course, if co-counsel will not speak again, the advocate must respond in the best way possible.

The advocate must maintain the argument's organization in the face of questions from the bench. Even the most inquisitive panels may permit the advocate to adhere to a basic organization if answers can be related to the contentions advanced. An advocate who permits the court to do the leading gives up the initiative, which may result in not fully developing intended arguments.

5. Transitions

After answering the question, the advocate will then return to the prepared extemporaneous argument. The transition should serve to direct the court's attention to the next point in the outline, while showing its relationship to the immediately preceding response. In the following example, the advocate smoothly directs the court's attention to the next point in the presentation:

> Q: And what is your definition of a RICO enterprise?

> A: It is this court's definition in *United States v. Turkette*. An association in fact proves by a common purpose and an ongoing organization. In this case, Mr. Burton and Ms. Younger are just such an association in fact. Furthermore, this association has injured Mr. Vitas to the extent of his losing $650,000. This injury is clearly within the reach of § 1964(c). The RICO injury requirement.

D. SUMMARY AND CONCLUSION

Toward the end of an argument, the advocate will usually discover that there are some contentions which have not been fully covered. At this point, the advocate will want to bring these issues to the court's attention by quickly summarizing them and inviting the court to their discussion in the written brief. And, if a relatively minor point has been subjected to lengthy inquiry, the advocate should place that point in its proper perspective.

Finally, the advocate will conclude the presentation. The conclusion will normally repeat the thesis statement of the argument and then ask the court to grant the relief requested in the written brief. However, the theme should change if the hearing reveals concerns of the court that could be more important in deciding the case:

> A: Mr. Vitas has alleged all the necessary elements of RICO cause of action. RICO applies to all individuals equally and be-

cause this is a 12(b) motion, the facts in
the complaint must be construed in a light
favorable to Mr. Vitas. Mr. Vitas is entitled to his day in court. Thank you.

E. REBUTTAL

Generally, it is wise for the advocate for the moving party to
reserve a short amount of time for rebuttal. Rebuttal provides the
advocate with the opportunity to reinforce arguments and leave a
favorable last impression with the court by rebutting the arguments
made by opposing counsel.

The rebuttal speech is short, and thus is limited to an attack on a
few key points raised by the opposition. The rebuttal is actually
prepared at the oral hearing. It is designed as a response to all that
has previously occurred at the hearing, including the presentations of
both sides, the judges' questions, and the advocate's answers.

The rebuttal should be focused, but the focus of each rebuttal must
evolve from the dynamics of the particular hearing. The advocate may
touch on those arguments which the court found appealing. Additionally, the advocate should concentrate on opposing counsel's strong
points or on glaring weaknesses in his or her own previous presentation. The rebuttal should conclude with a summary of the advocate's
contentions, an affirmative reiteration of the dispositive issues, and a
prayer for relief.

IV. SPEAKING STYLE

Perhaps the most difficult element of oral argument to prepare is
one's personal speaking style. This aspect of the advocate's oral argument develops only after lengthy practice and speaking experience.
Nonetheless, there are certain components of presentation which, if
perfected, will increase a presentation's persuasiveness. In particular,
the advocate should cultivate poise, persuasive use of voice and language, and a proper attitude.

A poised advocate exudes a confident, professional demeanor. Appropriate grooming and attire immeasurably aid in creating this impression. The best interests of the client will not be served if the
advocate distracts the court with a sloppy personal appearance and
casual dress. Likewise, an advocate's demeanor is reflected in personal
mannerisms in the courtroom. Certain affectations should always be
avoided: pounding on the lectern, slouching, pacing, and pointing at
the judges substantially detract from the advocate's presentation.

On the other hand, certain mannerisms aid the advocate in persuading the court. The advocate should strive to develop a personal
link with each of the judges through eye contact. Appropriate, natural

gestures complement the oral presentation. Also, as a courtesy both to the court and to opposing counsel, the advocate should remain quiet, attentive, and respectful while not at the podium.

Persuasive use of voice and language will also aid the advocate's presentation. Certain fundamentals of public speaking should be followed unhesitatingly. The voice should never sound forced, but the words should be clearly articulated. The flow of sentences should be emphasized by voice inflection and variation in pace and volume.

The appellate tribunal is not immune from boredom, and it is most difficult for judges to give unflagging attention to every legal contention presented. In order to arouse the court's interest, the advocate should make every effort to use an interesting vocabulary when addressing the court. At the same time, however, the advocate should avoid using terms in the vernacular; the court is a forum which deserves a formal oral presentation. The advocate should make an effort to use proper legal terms when appropriate, in order to explain precisely the points to be made.

Finally, an oral presentation is most persuasive when the advocate is at once assertive and deferential. Just as an obsequious advocate may fail to convince the court, so too, an overly aggressive advocate may alienate the tribunal. The advocate should therefore guard against erring in these two extremes.

Perhaps the best exercise to develop a persuasive speaking style is to rehearse in front of a mirror. Practice making an entire oral presentation, including answers to imagined questions, while maintaining eye contact with your reflected image. Strive to deepen your voice, infusing it with force and conviction. Above all, remember that you are an individual. The court will be more easily persuaded by your own style, than by what you imagine to be the "correct" technique.

APPENDIX A

BRIEF FOR PETITIONER FILED IN THE CASE OF VITAS v. YOUNGER & BURTON

———

IN THE

SUPREME COURT OF THE UNITED STATES

OCTOBER TERM 1983

No. 83-456

ROCKY VITAS,

Petitioner,

- AGAINST -

LORETTA YOUNGER and MICHAEL BURTON,

Respondents.

ON WRIT OF CERTIORARI
TO THE UNITED STATES COURT OF APPEALS
FOR THE THIRTEENTH CIRCUIT

BRIEF FOR THE PETITIONER

Susan Keller
Sally Helppie
Counsel for Petitioner
UCLA School of Law
405 Hilgard Avenue
Los Angeles, California 90024
(213) 825-1128

[D5896]

QUESTIONS PRESENTED

I.   Whether shares of ordinary corporate stock, carrying such traditional attributes, should be considered "securities" under the language of the relevant statutes and legislative history, and the appropriate "economic reality" examination.

II.   Whether traditional securities, purchased for an investment purpose, should be subject to the Howey test and the proposed "Sale of Business" doctrine.

III.   Whether an "organized crime" requirement should be read into RICO, despite an express congressional refusal to create such a status crime.

IV.   Whether the Petitioner, who has alleged that he has been injured as a result of racketeering acts committed by the respondents' enterprise, has stated a cognizable RICO cause of action.

[D5897]

TOPICAL INDEX

[D5898]

[D5899]

[D5900]

TABLE OF AUTHORITIES

[D5903]

                                                              [D5904]

Page

[D5905]

IN THE

SUPREME COURT OF THE UNITED STATES

OCTOBER TERM 1983

No. 83-456

ROCKY VITAS,

Petitioner,

— AGAINST —

LORETTA YOUNGER and MICHAEL BURTON,

Respondents.

ON WRIT OF CERTIORARI
TO THE UNITED STATES COURT OF APPEALS
FOR THE THIRTEENTH CIRCUIT

BRIEF FOR THE PETITIONER

OPINIONS BELOW

The opinion and order of the United States District court for the District of Arcana is unreported, and is contained in the Transcript of Record. (R. 11-16). The opinion of the United States Court of Appeals

[D5906]

for the Thirteenth Circuit is unreported, and is contained in the
Transcript of Record (R. 17-24).

JURISDICTION

A Formal Statement of Jurisdiction has been omitted in accordance
with the rules of the U.C.L.A. Moot Court Honors Program.

STATUTES INVOLVED

The text of the following statutes relevant to the determination of
the present case are set forth in the appendices: Securities Act of
1933, 15 U.S.C. § 77b(1) (1982); Securities Exchange Act of 1934, 15
U.S.C. §§ 78c(a)(10), 78j(b) (1982); Securities Exchange Commission
Rules, 17 C.F.R. 240.10b-5 (1983); Clayton Act, 15 U.S.C. § 15 (1982);
Organized Crime Control Act, P. L. 91-452, 84 Stat. 923 (1970);
Racketeer Influenced and Corrupt Organizations Act, 18 U.S.C. §§ 1961,
1962, 1964.

STATEMENT OF THE CASE

Petitioner Rocky Vitas is a self-employed professional tennis
player (R. 3). He purchased stock in Wholesale Computer, Inc. ("WCI"),
from Respondents Loretta Younger and Michael Burton, both former
directors, officers and shareholders of the company (R. 3). [D5907]

Mr. Vitas first met Ms. Younger on November 1, 1982, at which time Ms. Younger proposed that he buy her 100 shares of WCI stock. She represented that the corporation had operated profitably each year after 1977, that its profit for 1981 was in excess of $150,000, and that its prospects were very good. She further stated that Burton was completely responsible for all operations of the company, which depended upon his personal contacts for its success. Mr. Vitas would have no duties whatsoever with respect to WCI (R. 4). Younger explained that she wished to sell her shares in order to purchase an interest in a company that owned orange groves in Florida (R. 4).

In reliance upon Younger's representations, Mr. Vitas agreed to buy all her shares for $500,000, provided that he could also purchase at least 50 other shares. (Mr. Vitas had a total of $800,000 saved which he wished to invest.) Younger said that Burton would sell his 50 shares, provided Mr. Vitas continued Burton's long-term employment contract with the company. Mr. Vitas agreed. He pledged $150,000 for Burton's shares (R. 4).

On November 8, 1982, Mr. Vitas met with James Madison, the holder of the 50 remaining shares in WCI. Madison showed Mr. Vitas a letter which Younger had written stating: "All you'll have to do is sit back and let Mike Burton make your money work" (R. 5).

The purchase agreement contained warranties from Younger and Burton that they were unaware of any adverse developments concerning WCI occurring after June 30, 1982 (R. 6). At the closing, on November 22, Burton became Chair and President of the company, and--at his request--his annual bonus was increased to one-half of the company's

[D5908]

after-tax profit (R. 6). Mr. Vitas took no active role in the

management of the company (R. 6).

Mr. Vitas received the audited 1982 financial statements showing a

loss in excess of $50,000 on February 21, 1983 (R. 61). He questioned

Burton the next day, and Burton admitted that he had been seriously ill

since July 1982. This had drastically curtailed his effectiveness, and

was directly responsible for the company's financial loss. Burton had

confided in Younger the previous August, and she advised him to say

nothing. She told him she would bail them out (R. 7). Subsequently,

Younger developed the fraudulent scheme which enabled them to sell their

stock and invest together in Florida Oranges, Inc. (R. 7).

Mr. Vitas brought suit against Burton and Younger in the District

Court of Arcana. The first cause of action, alleging violations of

Section 10(b) of the Securities Exchange Act of 1934 and Rule 10b-5

promulgated thereunder, survived a motion to dismiss. The second,

predicated upon a violation of the Racketeer Influenced and Corrupt

Organizations Act of 1970 ("RICO") was dismissed pursuant to Fed. R.

Civ. P. 12(b)(6). On interlocutory appeal, the United States Court of

Appeals for the Thirteenth Circuit dismissed both causes of action.

Petitioner subsequently petitioned this Court for a writ of certiorari,

which was granted on July 18, 1983.

SUMMARY OF ARGUMENT

Petitioner Vitas has stated a valid claim under the Securities

Exchange Act of 1934. The shares of stock he purchased in Wholesale

[D5909]

Computer qualify as securities and come within the purview of federal securities laws and their special anti-fraud provisions.

"Stock" is a specifically enumerated "security" within the definitional sections of the 1933 and 1934 Acts. The factual context surrounding the purchase indicates that all the parties knew they were dealing with stock and were acquainted with its traditional attributes. Thus, Petitioner's expectation of coverage under federal securities laws is justifiable, especially considering Congress' intent that this remedial legislation be broadly construed to provide protection to investors in circumstances such as these. Additionally, a large body of case law espouses consideration of substance over form, examining the "economic reality" surrounding each instrument. Applying this analysis, Petitioner's stock qualifies as a security, given the presence of its traditional name and characteristic qualities and the absence of evidence that the buyer expected not to be covered.

Petitioner's purchase of stock meets all three prongs of the transactional "economic reality" analysis, as embodied by the Howey test for determining whether a transaction creates an investment contract. Thus, the Sale of Business Doctrine, which proposes to exempt transactions involving the transfer of all the shares of stock in a business from federal securities law jurisdiction, does not apply and should not be adopted by this Court.

Petitioner also has stated a valid claim under RICO. The plain language of RICO does not require that defendants be connected to organized crime. Moreover, Congress deliberately drafted RICO to apply

[D5910]

to <u>anyone</u> who commits racketeering acts. RICO proscribes <u>behavior</u>, not
status.

Further, Petitioner's complaint alleges at least three separate
RICO enterprises--Wholesale Computer, Florida Oranges, and Respondents'
"association in fact." Although Petitioner must allege both the
existence of an enterprise and a racketeering pattern, the proof need
not always be separate.

Additionally, the complaint plainly alleges that Petitioner has
suffered a $650,000 loss. Neither the statutory language nor the
legislative history suggest that RICO plaintiffs must suffer some
"special" injury. RICO requires only that there be a <u>causal connection</u>
between the racketeering acts and the harm suffered. Congress did not
intend for RICO remedies to be analogized to antitrust law. Such an
analogy is inappropriate considering the different goals and policies
underlying these two branches of law. Further, applying antitrust rules
to RICO could create insurmountable obstacles for plaintiffs, thus
leaving some targeted racketeering conduct unpunished.

Because Petitioner's complaint is before this Court on 12(b)(1) and
12(b)(6) motions, it should be reviewed in a light most favorable to
him. Mr. Vitas has sufficiently alleged violations of the Securities
Exchange Act and RICO, and he is entitled to his day in court.

[D5911]

ARGUMENT

I

PETITIONER'S SHARES OF STOCK IN WHOLESALE
COMPUTER, INC. ARE SECURITIES WITHIN THE
MEANING OF THE 1934 SECURITIES EXCHANGE ACT.

Petitioner's first cause of action is premised upon a violation of
Section 10(b) of the Securities Exchange Act of 1934 (the "1934 Act")
and S.E.C. Rule 10b-5 promulgated thereunder. 15 U.S.C. § 78j(b)
(1982); 17 C.F.R. 240.10b-5 (1983). See, Appendix B. Both of these
regulations concern the use of manipulative and deceptive devices or
contrivances in the purchase or sale of securities. Therefore, the
threshold consideration for situations involving a possible
violation--and the determination challenged by Respondents through their
motion to dismiss this claim--regards the presence of a "security," as
delineated by the Securities Exchange Act of 1934. See, Appendix A.
Petitioner's shares of stock in Wholesale Computer, Inc., clearly
qualify as "securities" under the definitional language of the statute,
as well as through the intent of Congress, and the relevant case law
which dictates examining the "economic reality" of and surrounding the
instrument itself.

    A.   DEFINITIONAL LANGUAGE OF THE SECURITIES ACTS
         INCLUDES "STOCK" AS AN ENUMERATED "SECURITY"

"The starting point in every case involving construction of a
statute is the language itself," Blue Chip Stamps v. Manor Drug Stores,

[D5912]

421 U.S. 723, 756 (1975). Section 3(a)(10) of the 1934 Act is

"virtually identical" to the definitional section of the Securities Act

of 1933 (The "1933 Act"), 15 U.S.C. § 77b(1) (1982), <u>Tcherepnin v.</u>

<u>Knight</u>, 389 U.S. 332, 336 (1967); both define the term "security" to

include commonly known documents traded for speculation or investment as

well as irregular instruments:

> [A]ny note, <u>stock</u>, treasury stock, bond, deben-
> ture, certificate of interest or participation
> in any profit-sharing agreement,. . .certificate
> of deposit for a security, or in general, <u>any</u>
> <u>instrument commonly known as a "security."</u>
> 15 U.S.C. § 78c(a)(10) (emphasis added).

Thus, "stock" falls squarely within the sepcifically enumerated

categories of "security."

1.   <u>Historically, corporate stock has been</u>
      <u>presumed covered by securities laws.</u>

In providing this definition, Congress sought to depict "security"

in sufficiently broad and general terms to provide the investor

reassurance and protection necessary in the aftermath of the disastrous

Stock Market "Crash" of 1929, and, particularly, "to include within

[the] definition the many types of instruments that in our commercial

world fall within the ordinary concept of a security." H. Rep. No. 85,

73d Cong., 1st Sess. 11 (1933). Then in 1943, this Court stated that

"[i]nstruments may be included within any of these definitions, as a

matter of law, if <u>on their face they answer to the name or description</u>."

<u>SEC v. C.M. Joiner Leasing Corp.</u>, 320 U.S. 344 (1943) (emphasis added).

This approach was reiterated in <u>Tcherepnin v. Knight</u>, 389 U.S. at 332

(D5913)

(withdrawable capital shares in savings and loan association were
"securities"); and <u>Joiner</u>'s validity was recently reaffirmed by this
Court in <u>Marine Bank v. Weaver</u>, 455 U.S. 551 (1982) (certificate of
deposit not "the ordinary concept of a security"). Thus, for almost
fifty years this Court has indicated that if something is called
"stock," the most commonly known and easily recognizable of the
enumerated instruments, then it should be considered a "security."
Stock purchasers and judicial interpreters have followed this premise:
"[W]hen a transaction involves stock, there is a strong presumption that
the statutes apply." <u>Occidental Life Ins. Co. v. Pat Ryan & Assoc.,
Inc.</u>, 496 F.2d 1255, 1261 (4th Cir. 1974).

    2.   <u>The factual context of this stock displays
all the characteristic attributes of
traditional securities instruments.</u>

The definitions in the 1933 and 1934 Acts are both preceded by the
phrase, "unless the context otherwise requires." 15 U.S.C., § 77b; 15
U.S.C. § 78c(a). Although some courts have taken a limited view of this
prefatory language, construing this term to refer to statutory context
within the Acts, the more recent interpretations refer to the factual
context of the instrument. <u>Marine Bank v. Weaver</u>, 455 U.S. at 556. The
factual context of the "stock" here at issue lends further support to
the finding that it is a "security." Respondents have conceded at oral
argument that the instruments in question "have all the attributes
commonly associated with ordinary corporate stock." <u>Vitas v. Younger</u>,

83 Civ. 1979, 13, n.1. (D. Arc.), aff'd in part, rev'd in part, No. 1853

(13th Cir. 1983). These attributes traditionally include: the name

given, negotiability, voting rights in proportion to number of shares

owned, right to receive dividends, and the possibility of appreciation

in value. Golden v. Garafalo, 678 F.2d 1139, 1143 (2d Cir. 1982),

quoting United Housing, Inc. v. Forman, 421 U.S. 837, 851, reh. denied

423 U.S. 884 (1975).

Petitioner purchased "stock" from Respondent Younger, referred to

at all times as the "majority shareholder" (R. 3, 4) and from Respondent

Burton, described as a "shareholder" in Wholesale Computer (R. 3, 4).

The record indicates that all the parties knew they were dealing with

"stock" and were acquainted with the characteristics of that instrument.

Under these circumstances, Petitioner's expectation of securities law

protection was entirely justified. It is totally inappropriate to

attribute ignorance or confusion to the parties in relation to this

instrument absent evidence that it existed.

> B.   SECURITIES LAW PROTECTION IS MANDATED
>   BY THE CONGRESSIONAL INTENT EVIDENCED
>   IN ENACTING THIS LEGISLATION.

The legislative history of the Acts demonstrates that Congress

wanted to protect investors from abuse in the financial markets. This

purpose was specifically articulated: "The aim [of the legislation] is

to prevent further exploitation of the public by the sale of unsound,

fraudulent, and worthless securities through misrepresentation."

[D5915]

S. Rep. 47, 73d Cong. 1st Sess. 1 (1933). Furthermore, this Court has emphasized that in interpreting the Acts, courts must be "guided by the familiar canon of statutory construction that remedial legislation should be construed broadly to effectuate its purposes." Tcherepnin v. Knight, 389 U.S. at 337. Therefore, without a clear showing that ordinary corporate stock is other than what it appears to be, Congress has mandated that investors be afforded the full coverage of the appropriate legislation. "The statutory policy of affording broad protection to investors is not to be thwarted by unrealistic and irrelevant formulae." SEC v. W.J. Howey, Co., 328 U.S. 293, 301 reh. denied, 329 U.S. 819 (1946).

This protection is not available only to those trading large amounts of registered securities on national exchanges. Congress chose to exempt small, private sales of stock from certain requirements under the Acts--such as registration--but specifically applied the Section 10(b) and Rule 10b-5 anti-fraud provisions to all stock. These prohibit manipulative and deceptive devices "in connection with the purchase or sale of any security registered on a national exchange or any security not so registered. . . ." 15 U.S.C. § 78j(b) (1982) (emphasis added).

> C.　THE "ECONOMIC REALITY" EXAMINATION ESPOUSED BY THE FORMAN OPINION REQUIRES NO TRANSACTIONAL INQUIRY WHEN TRADITIONAL INSTRUMENTS ARE INVOLVED.

A well-established body of case law urges disregarding "form for substance" and emphasizing "economic reality" to determine whether a

[D5916]

particular transaction is governed by securities legislation. These

notions were first introduced in SEC v. W.J. Howey Co., 328 U.S. 293

(1946), which involved land sales and service contracts for portions of

Floridan orange groves. This Court held that these were actually

"investment contracts"--included within the statutory definitions--and

outlined a three-pronged test to determine if the economic realities of

any given transaction justify finding it to be an investment contract.

Rather than expanding securities laws coverage as has been charged, this

Court actually was delineating a situation which did not involve a

conventional instrument but was clearly a "scheme devised by those

seeking the use of the money of others on the promise of profits."

Howey, 328 U.S. at 299. It was the very sort of situation in which

Congress had intended to provide investor protection.

This approach was applied and reaffirmed many times in cases

emphasizing that "in searching for the meaning and scope of the word

'security' in the Act, form should be disregarded for substance and the

emphasis should be on economic reality." Tcherepnin v. Knight, 389 U.S.

at 336. Through applying the Howey test, a wide variety of unusually

structured or uncommonly designated transactions have been found within

the reach of securities laws.

This Court's most extensive "economic reality" analysis is found in

United Housing Foundation, Inc., v. Forman, 421 U.S. 837 (1975), in

which shares of "stock" entitling purchasers to lease an apartment in a

state subsidized and supervised non-profit housing cooperative were

found not to be "securities" within the purview of the 1933 and 1934

Acts. This traditionally named instrument lacked all the common

[D5917]

characteristics usually associated with stock and did not satisfy the _Howey_ test for investment contracts. Thus, the economic realities of that situation justified denying the instrument coverage under the securities laws.

Subsequent confusion and controversy regarding the correct interpretation and application of the _Forman_ analysis have stemmed from careless readings of its well-reasoned opinion and inappropriate designations of the relevant tests. Lower courts have spoken of the "economic reality test," listing only the three prongs of the _Howey_ test for an investment contract, or referring only to the second half of the _Forman_ analysis as though _Forman_ does not urge an "economic reality" analysis in _all_ situations, with non-traditional _and_ conventional instruments. _See_, _e.g._, Frederiksen v. Poloway, 637 F.2d 1147 (7th Cir.), _cert. denied_, 451 U.S. 1017 (1981) (assets and stock in a marina); King v. Winkler, 673 F.2d 342 (11th Cir. 1982) (stock in a heating and air conditioning business).

Many courts have further muddled the examination by adding a subsequent analysis, applicable to situations involving sales of all the shares of or a controlling interest in a business. The resultant "Economic Realities Test/_Howey_ Test/Sale of Business Doctrine" hybrid is cumbersome to apply and leads to contradictory results. The instant case offers an ideal opportunity for this Court to separate and clarify the appropriate tests and doctrines, although a more conscientious reading of the _Forman_ opinion by lower courts might render this effort unnecessary.

[D5918]

1. Given ordinary corporate stock, only
    the first half of the Forman analysis
    is appropriate, absent evidence of the
    buyer's expectation not to be covered.

As securities laws coverage depends on the presence of an

enumerated instrument, consideration must begin with the instrument

involved, to see if its economic realities qualify it both in name and

fact as one of the securities listed in the Acts' definitions. If the

results of this examination are inconclusive--either because there is an

unusual instrument involved or because there is some indication of buyer

expectation not to be covered--then it is appropriate to look at the

economic realities of the transaction, to see if the instrument was

treated like a security or if the buyers are typical investors.

Thus, the two-part Forman analysis considered first the instrument,

then, after finding an absence of conventional characteristics, examined

the transaction. It is clear that this Court felt both analyses to be

of the inherent economic realities. In the first half of the opinion,

Justice Powell quotes Tcherepnin's admonition regarding consideration of

form, substance and "economic reality." In the second half of the

opinion he states: "In considering these claims we again must examine

the substance--the economic realities of the transaction." United

Housing v. Forman, 421 U.S. at 851 (emphasis added). Courts which

characterize the first consideration as an incomplete "literal test" are

ignoring Forman's specific rejection of a purely literal analysis. That

is, the name of an instrument alone is not dispositive. But a

traditional name in combination with all the characteristics commonly

[D5919]

associated with stock--in other words, the economic realities of that
instrument--dictates a presumption of "securities" status. In Forman,
the shares of "stock" did not entitle the holders to receive dividends,
were not negotiable, did not confer proportional voting rights, and were
not purchased with an anticipation of profits. Conversely, as conceded
by Respondents, the shares of stock in Wholesale Computer possess all
the common attributes of ordinary stock.

It is only reasonable to conclude that if something is called a
stock and appears to be a stock, it should be considered a security.
This conforms to standard practices in the business and investment
communities and is consistent with the expectations of those investors
who buy "stock." Even if purchasers are not acquainted with the entire
range and complexity of securities regulation, if they think it is
stock, they should be entitled to all the benefits and protections which
attach to securities. The only reason for not extending coverage would
be evidence of contrary buyer expectation which may be indicated by: a
sale of assets in a business as well as a transfer of stock, or an
agreement to sell a business before determining the method and structure
of the sale. See, infra, Sale of Business Doctrine discussion,
Section II B.

The Forman opinion specifically emphasizes the importance of buyer
expectation, stating that the mere name given to an instrument is not
"wholly irrelevant to the decision whether it is a security" because the
"use of a traditional name such as 'stock'. . . will lead a purchaser
justifiably to assume that the federal securities laws apply." The
opinion goes on to say that "[t]his would clearly be the case when the

[D5920]

underlying transaction embodies some of the significant characteristics typically associated with the named instrument." 421 U.S. at 851 (emphasis added).

In a situation involving ordinary corporate stock, it is only necessary to examine the economic realities of the instrument itself, as was demonstrated in the first half of the Forman analysis. When, as here, both a traditional name and significant characteristics typically associated with that name are present, there is an extremely strong presumption of coverage. The only mitigating factor would be clear-cut evidence of buyer expectation to the contrary. In this case, Petitioner's behavior and the information in the record are totally consistent with his justifiable expectation of coverage.

2.   The Howey test applies only to trans-
      actions involving investment contracts
      and other unusual instruments.

The Howey test for investment contracts is the relevant transactional economic realities analysis because it deals with how investment funds are handled. If the first economic realities consideration of the instrument is inconclusive--as it was in Forman--then the Howey test must be utilized. When investment funds are pooled into a "common enterprise," motivated by the investor's "expectation of profits" to be derived "solely from the efforts of others," then the transaction fits the securities mold, and the instrument can appropriately be deemed an investment contract.
[D5921]

SEC v. W.J. Howey, 328 U.S. 293, 301 (1946). If any of the three prongs
of the Howey test are not met, this would indicate that the funds were
not treated and/or the buyer and seller did not interact in a manner
consistent with intended securities laws coverage.

It is important to note that all the cases decided prior to Forman
which utilized the Howey test had involved unusual instruments. The
shares of "stock" in Forman could also be considered unusual, as they
lacked the traditional attributes of that instrument. But that was
determined only after looking at the economic realities of the "stock"
and noting its shortcomings. Thus, both parts of the analysis were
required in Forman. But if there is a traditionally named and
structured stock or other enumerated security, then there is no reason
to apply more than the first analysis; if the instrument is not
specifically enumerated or conventionally named then it is appropriate
to go straight to the Howey test.

Those courts which have interpreted the Howey test as being
relevant in all cases do so--once again--through a misreading of the
Forman opinion, in which the court states: "We perceive no distinction,
for present purposes, between an 'investment contract' and an
'instrument commonly known as a security.'" United Housing v. Forman,
surpa, 421 U.S. at 853. In other words, in that particular instance,
the Howey test determines whether a security is or is not present. The
"test, in shorthand form, embodies the essential attributes that [run]
through all of the Court's decisions defining a security" when an
unusual instrument was involved. 421 U.S. at 853.

[D5922]

II

EVEN APPLYING THE HOWEY ANALYSIS,
THE SALE OF WHOLESALE COMPUTER, INC.
STOCK SATISFIES ALL REQUIREMENTS.

The Thirteenth Circuit Court of appeals has followed that line of cases which incorrectly reads the Forman opinion as being first a "literalist" test and then an "economic reality" examination; it has subsequently applied the Howey test as the "economic reality" analysis and found the shares of Wholesale Computer not to be securities in the requisite sense. A careful reading of the Howey test, comparison with similar cases, and close examination of the facts in this particular situation, reveal that even if the Howey test is unnecessarily utilized, its requirements are fully satisfied.

A.   PETITIONER'S PURCHASE OF STOCK MEETS
      ALL THREE PRONGS OF THE HOWEY TEST.

The "common venture" requirement is met when there is a "sharing or pooling of funds." Hirk v. Agri-Research Council, Inc., 561 F.2d 96, 101 (7th Cir. 1977). The Seventh Circuit has further refined this element: "[F]or securities laws protection, the parties must be partic-ipant[s] in an enterprise whose profits were shared." Frederiksen v. Poloway, 637 F.2d at 1152. One quarter of the stock in Wholesale Computer is owned by James Madison (R. 5); Petitioner's funds were pooled with Madison's when he made the purchase. Additionally, after

[D5923]

the sale of stock, Burton's employment contract was modified to include
an annual bonus of one-half of the company's after-tax profits (R. 6).
Petitioner, Burton and Madison were participating in an enterprise with
shared profits. Thus, the Howey test first prong is met.

The second, "profit-expecting" prong is also satisfied. Petitioner
undoubtedly was motivated to purchase his shares in Wholesale Computer
by Younger's promise of large profits. In Forman, this Court found that
the second prong was not met, as purchasers there were attracted by "the
prospect of acquiring a place to live and not by financial returns on
their investments." United Housing v. Forman, 421 U.S. at 853. In
contrast, here Petitioner was enticed only by the lure of high return on
his investment.

Thirdly, Petitioner expected to derive these profits solely from
the efforts of Burton. The appropriate test for this prong has been
well articulated: "[W]hether the efforts made by those other than the
investor are the undeniably significant ones, those essential managerial
efforts which affect the failure or success of the enterprise." SEC v.
Glenn W. Turner Enterprises, Inc., 474 F.2d 476 (9th Cir.) cert. denied,
414 U.S. 821 (1973). Since he is not a business person, and is
uninitiated into the intricacies of sales of computers, Mr. Vitas was
doubtlessly tantalized by Younger's statements that Burton was
"completely responsible for all operations of the company and
"responsible for its success. . . ." (R. 5) "Under the circumstances,
Vitas agreed to buy Younger's shares (R. 12) and sought to invest all
his savings by buying an additional fifty shares, thus consolidating his
investment into one highly profitable source for which he would have

[D5924]

absolutely no responsibility. For a professional tennis player wishing
to concentrate on the demands of his own occupation, the chance to "sit
back and let Mike Burton make [his] money work" (R. 5) was irresistible.

After the sale, Mr. Vitas "took no active role in the management of
Wholesale Computer" (R. 6), confident that Burton, continuing in his
previous roles and taking on Younger's former responsibilities (R. 6),
would deliver as promised. Considering Petitioner's intent to remain a
passive investor and the extent of the deception perpetrated upon him by
Respondents, it would be shocking to deny Mr. Vitas the appropriate
anti-fraud protections of Section 10(b) and Rule 10b-5.

B.   THE SALE OF BUSINESS DOCTRINE IS NOT
     APPLICABLE UNDER THESE CIRCUMSTANCES.

As was pointed out in the Thirteenth Circuit opinion, some courts
deny federal securities laws coverage when the underlying transaction
involves the sale of a business rather than an "ordinary investment."
See, e.g., Frederiksen v. Poloway, 637 F.2d at 1147. This occurs in
situations which fail to satisfy either the first or third prong of the
Howey test: no common enterprise and/or the purchaser does not expect
his profits to come solely through the efforts of a third party. The
present instance does not qualify for consideration under the "Sale of
Business Doctrine," as it was demonstrably an ordinary investment, and
the relevant Howey test first and third prongs have been met. [D5925]

1.   Policy militates against the Supreme
      Courts adopting this doctrine.

The rationale behind the Sale of Business Doctrine has not been clearly articulated. Presumably, there is some concern about removing transactions involving ownership transfers in existing enterprises from the realm of securities laws in order to avoid inadvertently failing to comply with the registration and anti-fraud provisions required thereunder. This is a weak basis for carving wholesale exceptions out of securities laws jurisdiction. Those who do structure the transfer as a sale of stock gain the benefits of (1) a more favorable tax treatment, (2) relief from the liabilities associated with the enterprise, and (3) a method of avoiding transactional details associated with sales of assets. Seldin, When Stock is Not a Security: The "Sale of Business Doctrine" Under the Federal Securities Laws, 37 Bus. Law 637 (1982). Particular care in complying with registration requirements seems a small price to pay for the advantages and special protections afforded parties to securities transactions. But if this responsibility proves too burdensome, it is usually possible to structure the transfer as a sale of assets. When tangible property can be seen and inspected and when there is no transfer of liability, as with a sale of assets, the need for additional federal fraud protection is less compelling.

Looking closely at Frederiksen, the leading Sale of Business Doctrine exponent, it is apparent that the "purchase agreement" for the marina--involving a total price of $191,800 for the assets--was the primary instrument and the "stock purchase and voting trust agreement"--involving nominal consideration of $20--was merely a vehicle

[D5926]

transferring the business. 637 F.2d at 1149. In Chandler v. Kew Inc., 691 F.2d 443 (10th Cir. 1977), the sale of a liquor store entailed a transfer of assets and stock, the latter being merely an "indicia of ownership"; and in King v. Winkler, 673 F.2d 342 (11th Cir. 1982), the decision to structure the transfer as a sale of stock came after the agreement to sell the heating and air conditioning business. In all these situations in which the Sale of Business Doctrine was found to apply, the parties had the option of structuring the transfer as a sale of assets only.

The Sale of Business Doctrine embodies many shortcomings, creating ambiguities in application and result. Great difficulties arise in determining the control over the business and funds which is at the heart of the Howey test third prong, and many mixed questions of fact and law are involved in making this crucial finding. Asymmetrical results are possible, as when several minority shareholders sell to a single purchaser: only the latter would be denied protection, even though the buyer is most usually the victim if fraud is involved. See, Karjala, Realigning Federal And State Roles In Securities Regulation Through The Definition Of A Security, 1982 U. Ill. L.R. 413 (1982). It is far wiser to require parties to a sale to utilize an alternative structure than to create coverage exceptions which are unclear in extent and arbitrary in application.   [D5927]

2.   Even if accepted, the Sale of Business
      Doctrine is not appropriate in this case.

Hypothesizing the validity of the Sale of Business Doctrine and applying it to these circumstances as an academic exercise still does not bring this case within the parameters of the exception. Even overlooking that the Howey test first and third prongs are satisfied, this situation involves a sale of only seventy-five percent of the stock in Wholesale Computer. Petitioner made no effort to acquire the remaining twenty-five percent interest. And yet, almost all cases applying the Sale of Business Doctrine have involved the purchase of or clear-cut intent to purchase one hundred percent of the outstanding shares. For example, the recent Ninth Circuit ratification of the Sale of Business Doctrine concerned a sale of one hundred percent of the corporate stock in a saw milling business. Landreth Timber Co. v. Landreth, No. 81-3446, slip op. at 1315 (9th Cir. March 7, 1984). Sutter v. Groen, 687 F.2d 197 (7th Cir. 1982), provides the accepted alternative: the sale of more than fifty percent of a corporation's common stock created a rebuttable presumption of an entrepreneurship rather than an investment purpose. However, that presumption is clearly rebutted here by Petitioner's stated intent to invest in, but not manage, Wholesale Computers, Inc.

Reading all the facts against Petitioner rather than appropriately in his favor, at the very least Mr. Vitas must be accorded his day in court to satisfactorily rebut any lingering presumption that his purpose in buying stock in Wholesale Computer was not solely to make an

[D5928]

investment. Petitioner is an investor who is due and deserving of the coverage provided by federal securities laws, and he must have the option of that protection.

III

PETITIONER NEED NOT ALLEGE AN ORGANIZED
CRIME NEXUS TO STATE A RICO CAUSE OF ACTION.

The Racketeer Influenced and Corrupt Organizations Act ("RICO"), 18 U.S.C. §§ 1961-1968 (1982), establishes broad civil remedies for private plaintiffs. Under § 1964(c), "any person" injured by a violation of § 1962 "shall recover threefold the damages he sustains. . . ." See, Appendix D. Congress enacted RICO with the express provision that it be "liberally construed to effectuate its remedial purposes." Organized Crime Control Act ("OCCA"), Pub. L. No. 91-452 (1970), 84 Stat. 922, § 904(a).

In the instant case, the courts below dismissed Petitioner's RICO claim on the grounds that two of the necessary RICO elements had not been properly alleged: an enterprise "seperate [sic] and distinct from the alleged 'pattern of racketeering activity'" and a RICO injury "seperate [sic]. . . from that resulting from the commission of the predicate offenses." Vitas v. Younger, 83 Civ. 1979, 15 (D.Arc.), aff'd in part, rev'd in part, No. 1853 (13th Cir. 1983). Yet, neither court explained why Petitioner's complaint was insufficient.

"[A] complaint should not be dismissed for failure to state a claim unless it appears beyond doubt that the plaintiff would prove no set of

facts in support of his claim which would entitle him to relief."
Conley v. Gibson, 355 U.S. 41, 45-46 (1957) (emphasis added). Further,
the allegations must be reviewed in a light most favorable to the
plaintiff. De La Cruz v. Tormey, 582 F.2d 45, 48 (9th Cir. 1978),
cert. denied, 441 U.S. 965 (1979).

A.   RICO'S BROAD LANGUAGE DOES NOT REQUIRE THAT
     DEFENDANTS BE CONNECTED TO ORGANIZED CRIME.

The first step in interpreting a statute is to examine its
language. As this Court noted in a case construing RICO, in the absence
of a "clearly expressed legislative intent to the contrary, that
statutory language must ordinarily be regarded as conclusive." United
States v. Turkette, 452 U.S. 576, 581 (1981). This Court recently
reaffirmed that approach in another RICO case. See, Russello v. United
States, ___ U.S. ___, 104 S. Ct. 296, 299 (1983) (interpretation of
"interest" under § 1963(a)(1)).

RICO's language hardly could be more straightforward. There are
only three elements necessary for a valid RICO claim under 1964(c): (1)
a violation of § 1962 (which may be satisfied by alleging that "any
person associated with "any enterprise" affecting interstate commerce
acquired, invested or maintained an interest in, or conducted the
affairs of an enterprise through a pattern of racketeering activity);
(2) an injury to business or property; and (3) a causal connection
between the violation and the injury. See, Appendix D. Nowhere does
the statute even mention organized crime. Rather, it explicitly spells
out which acts, committed in what manner, are unlawful.

[D5930]

Yet, despite RICO's plain language, Respondents ask this Court to add an organized crime element to the statute. Although RICO was enacted primarily in <u>response</u> to organized crime, it was in no way <u>limited</u> to that problem. Indeed, Senator McClellan, one of RICO's chief sponsors, pointed out that "[i]t is impossible to draw an effective statute which reaches most of the commercial activities of organized crime, yet does not include offenses commonly committed by persons outside organized crime as well." 116 Cong. Rec. 18,940 (1970). Attempts by Respondents to graft an organized crime requirement onto the statute are contrary to Congress' intent. Congress enacted a broad statute, to be construed liberally; it is not up to the judicial system to narrow RICO.

As this court pointed out in <u>Diamond v. Chakrabarty</u>, 447 U.S. 303, 318 (1980) (citations omitted):

> We have emphasized in the recent past that '[o]ur individual appraisal of the wisdom or unwisdom of a particular [legislative] course. . .is to be put aside in the process of interpreting a statute. . . . Our task, rather, is the narrow one of determining what Congress meant by the words it used in the statute; once that is done our powers are exhausted.

If Congress had meant to limit RICO to defendants linked to organized crime, it would have done so. "[I]n § 3503(a) of Title VI of the [OCCA], Congress demonstrated that it knew how to limit a provision to 'a person who is believed to have participated in an organized criminal activity' if that was what was intended." <u>United States v. Aleman</u>, 609 F.2d 298, 303-4 (7th Cir. 1979), <u>cert. denied</u>, 445 U.S. 946 (1980) (two defendants convicted under RICO after committing three home burglaries). <u>See</u>, Appendix E. But Congress evidently did not intend for RICO to apply only to organized crime; it deliberately left out any

[D5931]

such words of limitation. And this court explicitly has stated that
"where Congress <u>includes</u> particular language in one section of a statute
but <u>omits</u> it in another section of the same Act, it is generally
presumed that Congress acts intentionally and purposely in the disparate
inclusion or exclusion." <u>Russello v. U.S.</u>, <u>supra</u>, 104 S.Ct. at 300,
citing <u>United States v. Wong Kim Bo</u>, 472 F.2d 720, 722 (5th Cir. 1972)
(emphasis added).

> B.   LEGISLATIVE HISTORY DEMONSTRATES THAT
>   CONGRESS DID NOT INTEND TO LIMIT RICO
>   TO DEFENDANTS LINKED TO ORGANIZED CRIME.

The language of RICO is clear and the legislative history further
emphasizes that there is no organized crime requirement. Congress knew
that RICO encompassed more than "mobsters." Indeed, Senator McClellan
specifically noted that RICO applied to <u>all</u> persons. "[If RICO] does not
violate the civil liberties of those who are engaged in organized crime,
it does not violate the civil liberties of those who are not engaged in
organized crime, but who nonetheless are within the incidental reach of
provisions primarily intended to affect organized crime." 116 Cong.
Rec. 18,914 (1970).

Thus, although RICO originally was conceived as an attack on
members of organized crime, Congress deliberately decided against
creating a status offense. Instead, RICO was designed to punish
<u>behavior</u>. Representative Poff, a RICO sponsor, explained that organized
crime "serve[s] simply as a shorthand method of referring to a large and
varying group of individual criminal <u>offenses</u> committed in diverse

[D5932]

circumstances." 116 Cong. Rec. 35,344 (1970) (emphasis added).

Further, the House explicitly <u>rejected</u> an amendment to RICO that would

have criminalized membership in the Mafia or La Cosa Nostra. 116 Cong.

Rec. 35,343 (1970) (suggestion of Rep. Biaggi defeated).

Congress was well aware that RICO would not be confined solely to

traditionally "organized crime." Indeed, Representative Mikva decried

the lack of a definition of organized crime and warned that, whatever

the statute's initial motives, "we will end up with cases involving all

kinds of things not intended to be covered. . . ." 116 Cong. Rec.

35,204 (1970). Further, Representative Eckhardt called the bill "a

monster" and predicted that it would [overload] the Federal courts by

moving large substantive areas of criminal law, formerly totally within

the police power of the State, into the Federal realm. . . ." 116 Cong.

Rec. 35,287; 35,288 (1970). Nonetheless, Congress passed the statute by

wide margins in both the House and Senate. 116 Cong. Rec. 972; 35,363.

        C.   THE MAJORITY OF FEDERAL APPELLATE COURTS HAVE
              REJECTED AN ORGANIZED CRIME REQUIREMENT.

Because both the language and legislative history of RICO emphasize

that the statue was aimed at behavior and not status, every federal

appellate court considering this issue has rejected a requirement that

defendants be tied to organized crime. In <u>Schacht v. Brown</u>, 711 F.2d

1343 (7th Cir. 1983), <u>cert.</u> <u>denied</u>, ____ U.S. ____, 52 U.S.L.W. 3423

(Nov. 28, 1983), the court allowed the Illinois Director of Insurance to

proceed with a civil RICO suit against the officers, directors and

parent corporation of an insurance company that was kept in business

past the point of insolvency. The <u>Schacht</u> court, citing numerous
federal district and appellate court cases as well as several law review
articles, emphasized that an organized crime requirement was
inappropriate. "Such an argument would, of course, be unavailing in
light of the clear decisions of this and other courts that application
of § 1962(c) is 'not restricted to members of organized crime.'"
<u>Schacht v. Brown</u>, <u>supra</u>, at 1353 (citations omitted).

Moreover, the reasoning of the district court in <u>Moss v. Morgan
Stanley</u>, 553 F. Supp. 1347 (S.D.N.Y.), <u>aff'd</u> 719 F.2d 5 (2d Cir. 1983),
on which the lower courts rely, was soundly criticized by the appellate
court. The second circuit, citing legislative history, expressly noted
that "[t]he language of the statute. . . does not premise a RICO
violation on proof or allegations of any connection with organized
crime." 719 F.2d at 7. Furthermore, RICO has been held applicable, and
a tie to organized crime has not been required, in a variety of other
situations. See, <u>e.g.</u>, <u>United States v. Forsythe</u>, 560 F.2d 1127, 1136
(3d Cir. 1977) (bribery of judges); <u>Owl Construction Co. v. Ronald Adams
Contractor, Inc.</u>, No. 83-3424, slip op. (5th Cir. March 23, 1984)
(inflation of invoices by construction materials supplier); <u>USACO Coal
Co. v. Carbomin Energy, Inc.</u>, 689 F.2d 94 (6th Cir. 1982) (corporate
promoter's breach of fiduciary duty); <u>Sutliff, Inc. v. Donovan
Companies</u>, No. 83-1308, 83-1499, slip op. (7th Cir. Feb. 9, 1984)
("bust-out" fraud against competing oil companies); <u>Bennett v. Berg</u>, 685
F.2d 1053, 1063, <u>aff'd en banc</u>, 710 F.2d 1361 (8th Cir. 1983) (operation
of retirement community through fraud): <u>United States v. Campanale</u>, 518
F.2d 352, 363 (9th Cir. 1975) <u>cert. denied sub nom.</u>, <u>Grancich v. United</u>

States 423 U.S. 1050 (1976) (extortion against meat packers). If this

Court now were to impose such a requirement, it would be doing what

Congress deliberately chose not to do.

Moreover, policy considerations militate against making membership

in an organized crime syndicate an element of a statute's violation.

First, an organized crime requirement could raise constitutional

questions. See, e.g., Robinson v. California, 370 U.S. 660 (1962)

(statute making status as narcotics addict a criminal offense violates

Fourteenth Amendment). Second, any definition that might withstand

constitutionality attacks could face charges of vagueness. Third, an

organized crime element could erect an insurmountable barrier for

plaintiffs--thus negating the statute's civil remedies. That criminal

conduct is more antisocial and dangerous when engaged in by persons

acting in concert, to further the goals of an ongoing organization, is

addressed by conspiracy law and the RICO "enterprise" requirement. It

is not necessary to add an organized crime element to RICO.

At any rate, in the instant case, Petitioner has alleged specific

acts of mail fraud, wire fraud and securities fraud. This pattern of

fraudulent conduct by Respondents is no less serious than "traditional"

organized criminal activity. There seems little justification for

allowing Respondents to elude the grasp of RICO merely because they do

not happen to belong to an established organized crime family.

[D5935]

IV

THE RICO CAUSE OF ACTION ADEQUATELY
ALLEGES BOTH A CONTINUING ENTERPRISE
AND A RICO INJURY.

Respondents have conceded that Mr. Vitas' complaint clearly alleges
the existence of RICO predicate acts, including mail fraud, wire fraud
and securities fraud (R. 15, n. 3), and that two or more predicate acts
within ten years of each other constitute a "pattern of racketeering
activity." 18 U.S.C. § 1961(5) (1982). Thus, the only issues in this
case are the presence of a RICO "enterprise" and a RICO "injury."

A.   PETITIONER HAS ALLEGED A RICO ENTERPRISE.

Respondents argue that a RICO enterprise must be demonstrated by
proof separate from that used to allege the predicate acts; but neither
the statute itself nor this court's interpretation of it support such a
claim. RICO defines "enterprise" as "any individual, partnership,
corporation, association, or other legal entity, and any union or group
of individuals associated in fact although not a legal entity."
18 U.S.C. § 1961(4) (1982) (emphasis added). This plain language
encompasses Petitioner's allegations.

The complaint alleges that Wholesale Computer is a corporation with
headquarters in the State of Arcana and representative offices in four
other states (R. 3). This establishes not only a RICO enterprise but a
connection to interstate commerce.

[D5936]

Moreover, the complaint alleges a <u>second</u> enterprise--an "association in fact" between Younger and Burton. (R. 9). Mr. Vitas has charged that both Respondents served as directors and officers of Wholesale Computer (R. 3,6). He has alleged that Respondents acted in concert to conceal the true value of the Wholesale Computer shares. Further, he has alleged that both Respondents used the proceeds from the sale of their shares to acquire interests in yet another enterprise, Florida Oranges, Inc. (R. 8). Petitioner's allegations plainly state the existence of at least one RICO enterprise.

Petitioner's allegations also fulfill the test for a RICO enterprise which was articulated by this court in <u>United States v. Turkette</u>, 452 U.S. 576 (1981). (Although <u>Turkette</u> was a criminal case, its test is equally appropriate in a civil context--and the lower courts have applied it that way.) In <u>Turkette</u>, the indictment described the enterprise as "a group of individuals associated in fact for the purpose of illegally trafficking in narcotics,. . .committing arsons, [etc.]. . . ." 452 U.S at 579. This court explicitly held that the term "enterprise" includes both legitimate and illegitimate entities. 452 U.S. at 580. It then went on to define a RICO enterprise as "an entity, for present purposes a group of persons associated together for a common purpose of engaging in a course of conduct. . .proved by evidence of an ongoing organization, formal or informal, and by evidence that the various associates function as a continuing unit." 452 U.S. at 583.

Here, Respondents joined forces in 1975 to work together to earn a profit. The association began with the operation of Wholesale Computer;

[D5937]

when that was no longer profitable, the association unloaded its shares
and continued to fulfill its common purpose through an investment in
Florida Oranges (R. 3,4,6,7). At all times, the association functioned
as a separate entity. It was not formed to conduct acts of mail fraud,
wire fraud and securities fraud; on the contrary, the entity developed
and operated as a means of fulfilling the members' common purpose: to
make money.

When Burton told Younger in August of 1982 that he was ill and
could no longer operate Wholesale Computer profitably, Younger told him
that she would "bail [them] out" (R. 7). Instead of ending their
association, Younger devised a scheme whereby the two could continue
operating their enterprise. Both Respondents subsequently sold their
Wholesale Computer shares to Mr. Vitas and invested in Florida Oranges.
Respondents created, and continued to operate as, a stable unit.

The Younger-Burton enterprise is separate and distinct from the
racketeering acts the individuals committed. While plaintiffs must
demonstrate both an enterprise and a pattern of racketeering activity,
this Court has noted that "the proof used to establish these separate
elements may in particular cases coalesce. . . ." U.S. v. Turkette, 452
U.S. at 585. Nonetheless, Petitioner has alleged separate facts to show
each element.

Allegations of an enterprise in this case are even more clear than
evidence which has proved sufficient in prior cases. In United States
v. Errico, 635 F.2d 152 (2d Cir. 1980), cert. denied, 453 U.S. 911
(1981), a horse race fixing case, the court found an enterprise even
though many of the group's members changed. Further, in United States

[D5938]

v. <u>Griffin</u>, 660 F.2d 996 (4th Cir. 1981), <u>cert.</u> <u>denied</u>, 454 U.S. 1156
(1982), the court ruled that a group of individuals who separately
bribed police officers, to protect their own gambling operations,
constituted an association in fact. And in the <u>Turkette</u> case itself,
this court found an enterprise where one man committed a series of
crimes with a changing group of accomplices. 452 U.S. at 580.

Here, the Younger-Burton enterprise included the same personnel
over the years. It operated as a single unit with a common purpose.
Indeed, the enterprise continues to operate through Florida Oranges.
When Congress imposed an enterprise requirement for RICO violations, it
recognized that criminals often are more dangerous when they act in
concert. In this case, neither Burton nor Younger could have executed
their schemes alone. Burton was the operating force behind Wholesale
Computer while it was profitable, and Younger masterminded the plan to
dispose of the company after Burton's illness was discovered. In order
to successfully extricate themselves from Wholesale Computer, <u>both</u>
Respondents made misrepresentations and concealed material facts. Thus,
the "association in fact," which remains a viable entity, enabled them
to deceive Mr. Vitas.

Petitioner has alleged the existence of two legitimate enterprises
and one association in fact. Not only do his allegations fall within
the clear language of RICO, but they additionally satisfy the standard
enunciated by this court in <u>Turkette</u>.

[D5939]

B.   PETITIONER HAS ALLEGED A RICO INJURY.

RICO provides that "<u>any person</u> injured in his business or property
by reason of a violation of Section 1962. . .may sue therefor. . .and
<u>shall</u> recover threefold the damages he sustains and the cost of the
suit. . . ." 18 U.S.C. § 1964(c) (1982) (emphasis added). The statute
does not limit recovery to some sort of "special" injury; rather, it
expressly states that any person harmed shall recover. Mr. Vitas has
suffered severe financial losses by reason of Respondents' pattern of
fraudulent conduct and is entitled to civil damages under RICO.

The courts below, however, dismissed Mr. Vitas' complaint because
he failed to allege an injury distinct from that resulting from the
commission of the predicate offenses. Yet the courts did not explain
what sort of injuries would be sufficient to satisfy this extra burden.

    1.   <u>RICO does not require an injury separate and
          distinct from the injury that results from the
          predicate offenses</u>.

RICO's language is clear: if a private person is harmed by a
violation of § 1962, he <u>shall</u> <u>recover</u> treble damages. Yet, some lower
courts have tried to judicially limit this provision by adding a
"special" injury requirement. Such attempts are inappropriate judicial
excursions into legislative matters. As Justice Frankfurter has noted:

> A judge must not rewrite a statute, neither to enlarge
> nor to contract it. Whatever temptations the Statesmanship
> of policy making might wisely suggest, construction must
> eschew interpolation and evisceration. He must not read
> in by way of creation. He must read out except to avoid
> patent nonsense or internal contradiction.
>   [D5940]

Frankfurter, Some Reflections on the Reading of Statutes, 47 Colum. L.

Rev. 527, 533, (1947), cited in Blakey, The RICO Civil Fraud Action in

Context: Reflections on Bennett v. Berg, 58 Notre Dame L. Rev. 237,

285, n. 145 (1982). The district court ignored this warning and

judicially added a special-injury requirement onto Petitioner's RICO

claim.

The RICO injury element does require a causal connection between

the predicate acts and the loss suffered by a RICO plaintiff. Congress

may have inserted this requirement because otherwise some defendants

could be civilly liably for making a series of false representations as

to the value of securities even if the purchaser did not rely on the

misrepresentations. Thus, a RICO plaintiff must prove some injury to

recover--but neither the statute itself nor the legislative history

support the addition of anything more.

2.   RICO is not analogous to antitrust law.

Lower courts which have required anticompetitive or commercial RICO

injuries generally analogize the statute to antitrust law. See, e.g.,

Landmark Savings Loan v. Rhoades, 527 F. Supp. 206 (E.D. Mich. 1981)

(plaintiffs must allege a "racketeering enterprise" injury analogous to

an antitrust injury). These courts rely on the mere use of the same

three words (i.e., "by reason of") in the treble damages sections of

both RICO and the Clayton Act. See, Appendices D, F. This analysis is

misguided. First, the proposed legislation which preceded the OCCA was

originally offered as an addition to antitrust law, but Congress

[D5941]

explicitly rejected such a tie. Blakey, supra, 58 Notre Dame L. Rev. at

285. Congress followed the American Bar Association's ("ABA")

recommendation that the anti-crime bill be placed in a separate statute

to avoid the "commingling of criminal enforcement goals with the goals

of regulating competition. . . ." Blakey, supra at 285.

Further, shortly after introducing OCCA and RICO, Senator McClellan

emphasized that there was "no intention. . .of importing the great

complexity of antitrust law enforcement into this field." 115 Cong.

Rec. 9567 (1969). Heeding Senator McClellan's words, the "greater

number of courts which have reviewed RICO have reiterated that a

competitive injury is not necessary. Schacht v. Brown, 711 F.2d 1343

(7th Cir. 1983) cert. denied, ___ U.S. ___, 52 U.S.L.W. 3423 (Nov. 28,

1983). See, also, Bennett v. Berg, 685 F.2d 1053, 1059, aff'd en

banc, 710 F.2d 1361 (8th Cir. 1983) ("[A]lthough RICO borrowed the tools

of antitrust law to combat organized criminal activity, we do not

believe the RICO Act was limited to the antitrust goal of preventing

interference with free trade.")

Moreover, the list of RICO predicate offenses includes a number of

acts that "clearly do not render a competitive advantage, such as

bankruptcy fraud, dealing in narcotics or other dangerous drugs,

embezzlement of union funds, welfare fraud and the like." MacIntosh,

Racketeer Influenced and Corrupt Organization Act: Powerful New Tool of

the Defrauded Securities Plaintiff, 31 U. Kan. L. Rev. 57 (1982) (citing

18 U.S.C. § 1982)). If Congress intended to avoid RICO's application to

"garden variety" fraud claims, it could have removed mail, wire and

[D5942]

securities fraud from the list of racketeering activities. Schacht v.

Brown, supra, 711 F.2d at 1356.

Additionally, importing antitrust law into the RICO arena would

erect an unjustified barrier for civil plaintiffs. "Such a private

litigant would have to contend with a body of precedent--appropriate in

a purely antitrust context--setting strict requirements on questions

such as 'standing to sue' and 'proximate cause.'" ABA Report, cited in

Blakey, 58 Notre Dame L. Rev. at 255, n. 52.

Furthermore, requiring an antitrust injury would leave some

targeted behavior unpunished. If only those plaintiffs who suffered

competitive injuries had standing to sue, certain racketeering

enterprises could escape civil liability. As the plaintiffs in one case

asked, "[w]ho would have standing to sue a group of racketeers engaged

in a pattern of arson fraud? The gangsters' competition?" Kimmel v.

Peterson, 565 F. Supp. 476, 495, n. 23 (E.D. Pa. 1983).

Perhaps most importantly, different goals and policies underlie

RICO and antitrust law. Antitrust law is meant to halt anticompetitive

activity. But RICO is designed to "divest the association of the fruits

of its ill-gotten gains." U.S. v. Turkette, supra, 452 U.S at 585.

> [T]his purpose would be severely undermined if persons who
> suffered direct harm from racketeering activity. . .could not
> recover in the absence of a showing of some 'special'
> harm. . . . Such a rule would leave money derived from
> actions prohibited by RICO precisely where Congress did not
> intend it to remain, in the hands of RICO violators.

Crocker Nat'l Bank v. Rockwell Int'l Corp., 555 F. Supp. 47, 49-50 (N.D.

Cal. 1982).

Respondents suggest that Mr. Vitas does not "need" RICO as he has

sufficient remedies for fraud under state law and federal securities

[D5943]

law. But Congress explicitly included securities fraud within the list
of RICO predicate offenses, knowing full well that it was providing
additional remedies to those injured under certain circumstances.
Congress intended the treble damages remedy to serve as an extra tool to
reach criminals who operate through an enterprise. As this court has
recognized, "[t]he legislative history clearly demonstrates that the
RICO statute was intended to provide new weapons of unprecedented scope
for an assault upon organized crime and its economic roots." Russello
v. U.S., ____ U.S. ____, 104 S. Ct. at 302 (emphasis added). Further,
Respondents here have committed more than a single "garden variety"
fraud. It is good policy to provide stiffer sanctions, through RICO,
against those who use an enterprise to commit a series of deliberate
frauds.

        C.   IF RICO NEEDS LIMITATIONS, IT IS CONGRESS'
            RESPONSIBILITY TO ENACT THEM.

Restrictions upon RICO's broad provisions should not be judicially
imposed. As Justice Krook emphasized in his dissenting opinion in this
case, "we are not free to substitute our views for those of Congress
where Congress has spoken clearly." Vitas v. Younger, No. 1853, 23
(13th Cir. 1983). And RICO's language hardly could be clearer; it
specifies particular remedies for particular unlawful conduct. It is
not up to the judiciary to add requirements of special injuries and
links to organized crime. As this Court succinctly stated: "The short
answer is that Congress did not write the statute that way." United
States v. Naftalin, 441 U.S. 768, 773 (1979) (interpretation of

§ 17(a)(1) of the Securities Act of 1933). If there are practical problems with RICO that Congress did not foresee, that would be an appropriate matter for legislative action.

Petitioner has alleged the essential elements of a RICO claim and should be allowed to prove his case in court.

CONCLUSION

For the reasons set forth, Petitioner respectfully requests that the judgment of the United States Court of Appeals for the Thirteenth Circuit be reversed, and that Respondents' motions to dismiss the first cause of action for lack of federal subject matter jurisdiction and to dismiss the second cause of action for failure to state a claim be denied.

Respectfully submitted,

_____
Susan Keller

_____
Sally Helppie
Attorneys for Petitioner

[D5945]

APPENDIX A

Securities Act of 1933:

15 U.S.C. § 77b(1) (1982):

2.   When used in this title, unless the context otherwise
      requires--

      (1)   The term "security" means any note, stock, treasury
            stock, bond, debenture, evidence of indebtedness,
            certificate of interest or participation in any
            profit-sharing agreement, collateral-trust certificate or
            subscription, transferable share, investment contract,
            voting-trust certificate, certificate of deposit for a
            security, fractional undivided interest in oil, gas, or
            other mineral rights, or, in general, any interest or
            instrument commonly known as a "security" . . . .

Securities Exchange Act of 1934:

15 U.S.C. § 78c(a)(10) (1982):

3.   (a)   When used in this title, unless the context otherwise
            requires--

            . . . .

      (10) The term "security" means any note, stock, treasury
            stock, bond, debenture, certificate of interest or
            participation in any profit-sharing agreement, or in any
            oil, gas, or other mineral royalty or lease, any
            collateral-trust certificate, preorganization certificate
            or subscription, transferable share, investment contract,
            voting-trust certificate, certificate of deposit, for a
            security, or in general, any instrument commonly known as
            a "security"; or any certificate of interest or
            participation in, temporary or interim certificate for,
            receipt for, or warrant or right to subscribe to or
            purchase, any of the foregoing; but shall not include
            currency or any note, draft, bill of exchange, or
            banker's acceptance which has a maturity at the time of
            issuance of not exceeding nine months, exclusive of days
            of grace, or any renewal thereof the maturity of which is
            likewise limited.

                                                              [D5946]

APPENDIX B

Securities Exchange Act of 1934:

15 U.S.C. § 78j (1982): Manipulative and deceptive devices

It shall be unlawful for any person, directly or indirectly, by the
use of any means or instrumentality of interstate commerce or of
the mails, or of any facility of any national securities exchange--

(a) To effect a short sale, or to use or employ any stop-loss
    order in connection with the purchase or sale, of any security
    registered on a national securities exchange, in contravention
    of such rules and regulations as the Commission may prescribe
    as necessary or appropriate in the public interest or for the
    protection of investors.
(b) To use or employ, in connection with the purchase or sale of
    any security registered on a national securities exchange or
    any security no so registered, any manipulative or deceptive
    device or contrivance in contravention of such rules and
    regulations as the Commission may prescribe as necessary or
    appropriate in the public interest or for the protection of
    investors.

Securities Exchange Commission Rules:

17 C.F.R. 240.10b-5 (1983): Employment of manipulative and deceptive
    devices.

It shall be unlawful for any person, directly or indirectly, by the
use of any means or instrumentality of inter-state commerce, or of
the mails or of any facility of any national securities exchange,

(a) To employ any device, scheme, or artifice to defraud.
(b) To make any untrue statement of a material fact or to omit to
    state a material fact necessary in order to make the
    statements made, in the light of the circumstances under which
    they were made, not misleading, or

(c) To engage in any act, practice, or course of business which
    operates or would operate as a fraud or deceit upon any
    person, in connection with the purchase or sale of any
    security.   [D5947]

APPENDIX C

18 U.S.C. § 1961 (1982) provides in relevant part:

As used in this chapter—

(1) 'racketeering activity" means (A) any act or threat involving murder, kidnaping, gambling, arson, robbery, bribery, extortion, or dealing in narcotic or other dangerous drugs, which is chargeable under State law and punishable by imprisonment for more than one year; (B) any act which is indictable under any of the following provisions of title 18, United States Code: Section 201 (relating to bribery), section 224 (relating to sports bribery), sections 471, 472, and 473 (relating to counterfeiting), section 659 (relating to theft from interstate shipment) if the act indictable under section 659 is felonious, section 664 (relating to embezzlement from pension and welfare funds), sections 891–894 (relating to extortionate credit transactions), section 1084 (relating to the transmission of gambling information), section 1341 (relating to mail fraud), section 1343 (relating to wire fraud), section 1503 (relating to obstruction of justice), section 1510 (relating to obstruction of criminal investigations), section 1511 (relating to the obstruction of State or local law enforcement), section 1951 (relating to interference with commerce, robbery, or extortion), section 1952 (relating to racketeering), section 1953 (relating to interstate transportation of wagering paraphernalia), section 1954 (relating to unlawful welfare fund payments), section 1955 (relating to the prohibition of illegal gambling businesses), sections 2314 and 2315 (relating to interstate transportation of stolen property), sections 2341–2346 (relating to trafficking in contraband cigarettes), sections 2421-24 (relating to white slave traffic); (C) any act which is indictable under title 29, United States Code, section 186 (dealing with restrictions on payments and loans to labor organizations) or section 501(c) (relating to embezzlement from union funds); or (D) any offense involving fraud connected with a case under title 11, fraud in the sale of securities, or the felonious manufacture, importation, receiving, concealment, buying, selling, or otherwise dealing in narcotic or other dangerous drugs, punishable under any law of the United States;

(3) "person" includes any individual or entity capable of holding a legal or beneficial interest in property;

(4) "enterprise" includes any individual, partnership, corporation, association, or other legal entity, and any union or group of individuals associated in fact although not a legal entity;

(5) "pattern of racketeering activity" requires at least two acts of racketeering activity, one of which occurred after the effective date of this chapter and the last of which occurred within ten years (excluding any period of imprisonment) after the commission of a prior act of racketeering activity;

[D5949]

APPENDIX D

18 U.S.C. § 1962 (1982) provides in relevant part:

(a) It shall be unlawful for any person who has received any income derived, directly or indirectly, from a pattern of racketeering activity or through collection of an unlawful debt..., to use or invest, directly or indirectly, any part of such income, or the proceeds of such which is engaged in, or the activities of which affect, interstate or foreign commerce....

(b) It shall be unlawful for any person through a pattern of racketeering activity or through collection of any unlawful debt to acquire or maintain, directly or indirectly, any interest in or control of any enterprise which is engaged in, or the activities of which affect, interstate or foreign commerce.

(c) It shall be unlawful for any person employed by or associated with any enterprise engaged in, or the activities of which affect, interstate or foreign commerce to conduct or participate, directly or indirectly, in the conduct of such enterprise's affairs through a pattern of racketeering activity or collection of unlawful debt.

18 U.S.C. § 1964(c) (1982) provides:

Any person injured in his business or property by reason of a violation of Section 1962 of this chapter may sue therefor in any appropriate United States district court and shall recover threefold the damages he sustains and the cost of the suit, including a reasonable attorney's fee.

[D5950]

APPENDIX E

Organized Crime Control Act
Title VI
18 U.S.C. § 3503(a)

§ 3503. Depositions to preserve testimony

   (a) Whenever due to exceptional circumstances it is in the
interest of justice that the testimony of a prospective witness of a
party be taken and preserved, the court at any time after the filing of
an indictment or information may upon motion of such party and notice to
the parties order that the testimony of such witness be taken by
deposition and that any designated book, paper, document, record,
recording, or other material not privileged be produced at the same time
and place. If a witness is committed for failure to give bail to appear
to testify at a trial or hearing, the court on written motion of the
witness and upon notice to the parties may direct that his deposition be
taken. After the deposition has been subscribed the court may discharge
the witness. A motion by the Government to obtain an order under this
section shall contain certification by the Attorney General or his
designee that the legal proceeding is against a person who is believed
to have participated in an organized criminal activity . . . .

                                                    [D5951]

APPENDIX F

15 U.S.C. § 15 (1982) provides in relevant part:

   (a) Amount of recovery; prejudgment interest

   Except as provided in subsection (b) of this section, any
person who shall be injured in his business or property by reason
of anything forbidden in the antitrust laws may sue therefor in any
district court of the United States in the district in which the
defendant resides or is found or has an agent, without respect to
the amount in controversy, and shall recover threefold the damages
by him sustained, and the cost of suit, including a reasonable
attorney's fee.

                                                    [D5952]

Appendix B

TRANSCRIPT OF PETITIONER'S ORAL ARGUMENT IN VITAS v. YOUNGER & BURTON

A: May it please the Court, I am Sally Helppie, counsel for the Petitioner. This afternoon I will be explaining why petitioner's complaint adequately alleges a RICO cause of action.

Your Honor, Mr. Vitas has alleged all the necessary elements of a RICO claim. First, there is no organized crime element to speak of under RICO, and secondly, Mr. Vitas has alleged the existence of both an enterprise and an injury.

Your Honor, the Racketeering Influenced and Corrupt Organizations Act was enacted in 1970 as Title IX of the Organized Crime Control Act. When Congress began to develop this legislation it was searching for a new way of dealing with a nationwide problem. Your Honor, this Court has stated that in interpreting a statute the starting point is with the language of the statute itself. The RICO statute does not even mention the words organized crime. Yet the respondents ask this court to graft on an organized crime requirement primarily so that their clients would not be chargeable under it.

Q: It was the title of the bill, though.

A: Your Honor, certainly the title of the bill is the Organized Crime Control Act but when we look at the sections underneath that we can see that Title XI, for example, deals with the importation of explosives, which on its face does not directly relate to organized crime. Congress deliberately drafted a very broad bill here. There were a lot of problems across the nation with which Congress wished to deal and decided to develop a national approach to these problems. RICO was just one element under the Organized Crime Control Act, and RICO is the section which we wish to apply today. As I pointed out . . .

Q: But in your brief you quote legislative history saying that, as I read it, that they never intended to cover a smaller segment, simply organized crime; that most everybody is included in this. I don't know how good your authority is, but a representative Mikva decried the lack of a definition of organized crime, saying that we will end up with cases involving all kinds of things not intended to be covered.

A: Well, Your Honor, Representative Mikva did point out to Congress that this was a very broad section and may not be what Congress initially intended to cover. However, despite that warning, Congress went ahead and enacted RICO.

Q: What is that?

A: When Representative Biagghi suggested an amendment to the statute that would make membership in the Mafia or Costa Nostra criminal, Congress resoundingly defeated that. Instead Congress chose to outlaw behavior instead of status, and Congress included under the predicate acts section of RICO a sort of criminal activity that is commonly engaged in by traditional organized crime families. However, RICO clearly stated in Section 1962 that it is unlawful for any person to commit those predicate acts through the existence of an enterprise. Congress does not say it is unlawful for members of organized crime to commit these acts, but it is unlawful for any person.

Q: What does the enterprise require? Two people get together to defraud a third person to his detriment? Is that an enterprise?

A: No, Your Honor. This court set down a test in *United States v. Turkette.* A RICO enterprise is shown when there is an "association in fact." We are alleging here . . .

Q: That's included in my hypothetical. That's an enterprise.

A: Your Honor, we are alleging that is an association in fact with a common purpose, which is proved by its ongoing unit and continued organization.

Q: That's also included in my hypothetical. If it's ongoing over a period of a week or a month, does that meet the requirements?

A: Well, Your Honor, this court didn't specifically set down a definite number of days. In the case before this court the respondents teamed up together back in 1975. They've been together for nine years. Your Honor, that is more than enough time to . . .

Q: Yes, but they haven't been defrauding people since then.

A: Your Honor, the RICO enterprise element does not require that an enterprise only defraud people. What we have here is an enterprise, an association in fact that began with the common purpose of earning money. The respondents teamed up in 1975 to form Wholesale Computer.

Q: But not by defrauding?

A: No, they did not. Which makes it an even stronger enterprise.

Q: Was that the same enterprise? Was the business itself even during its halcyon days when they were doing well, and not defrauding people, was that the kind of enterprise contemplated by RICO?

A: Well, the business itself, Wholesale Computer, is not the enterprise we're alleging. It is the team of Burton and Younger, the association in fact, which has existed for nine years.

Q: So that there is a kind of a retroactive effect given to even their legal association.

A: Your Honor, an enterprise need not be engaged solely in illegal activities. The fact that it was involved in legal activities makes the existence of the enterprise that must stronger. It was not formed merely to conduct a series of predicate acts.

Q: (interrupting) Initially, like most businesses originally formed to make money.

A: Exactly. And they did, Your Honor.

Q: And as far as we know, legitimately.

A: For the first few years.

Q: But that is the beginning of the enterprise which subsequently becomes the illegal enterprise which comes under RICO, because of their later activities.

A: Well, Your Honor, RICO is not limited to purely illegal enterprise. In fact, that was the precise issue . . .

Q: Well, why did Congress want to make the availability of a federal forum and triple damages available to some frauds involving two people who are involved with one another in a lawful business for some period of time.

A: It was not the fact that they were associated together in an unlawful business. It is a fact that the two operated as a team. Evidence of the team's operation begins in 1975 and the team defrauded not only Mr. Vitas, but Mr. Madison through a series of deliberate frauds. The two are continuing there right now, investing together in Florida oranges.

Q: What is the ascertainable structure of this team? Do you recognize the words "ascertainable structure"?

A: Your Honor, this Court in *Turkette* did note that the structure could be loose or informal. It didn't have to have . . .

Q: But the meaning of the two words. Do they ring a bell as "ascertainable structure"? What case are they from?

A: Your Honor, I can't recall off the top of my head, but I would be happy to give you that information in a supplemental brief.

Q: Well, they are from the *Bledsoe* decision. Are you familiar with this case?

A: Yes, Your Honor. The *Bledsoe* case was a very close decision, a 2–1 decision.

Q: So it is not worth mentioning.

A: Well, that was an Eighth Circuit case which this Court is not bound to follow. But, Your Honor, even the *Bledsoe* decision noted that the structure and the roles did not have to be filled continuously by the same people. That would defeat the very purpose of RICO; because the leader of an organization then could bring in lower level associates and continually change these individual's roles for illegal purposes. If we're looking for an ascertainable structure here, we have two people who worked as a team.

Q: But when Younger sold her stock, she didn't try to push Burton's stock on Vitas. All of a sudden Vitas said "I want the other fifty shares. Where can I get them?"

A: Well, Your Honor, on a 12(b) motion, we have to look at the complaint in a light most favorable to Mr. Vitas. Mr. Vitas did have $800,000 that he wished to invest, and it's only natural that this property was represented to him so highly profitable that he would want to have as large a percentage of that business as he possibly could. His intent in wanting an additional fifty shares, not necessarily Mr. Burton's shares, just an additional fifty percent, was to have a higher percentage of the huge profits that were sure to be raked in.

Q: Suppose a group of players have a weekly poker game. Two of the players, one day, really want to strike it rich and bring in a marked deck and they really skin one of the players. Is there a RICO violation?

A: No, Your Honor, because it's not affected interstate commerce.

Q: One of the players is from out of state.

A: It still wouldn't necessarily be affecting interstate commerce.

Q: You mean, even if they called him on the telephone?

A: That would be a different fact situation than what we have before us today. It would possibly be the case if the two people who decided to defraud others had a separate organization themselves, and were not just part of a larger organization that was unaware that it was being considered a RICO enterprise. Your Honor, if it is unclear here, we would only like an opportunity to prove that the enterprise exists in court. Because of the dismissal, we were denied an opportunity to present our case to the trier of fact.

Q: But we have to provide a definition of what constitutes an enterprise.

A: Yes, Your Honor.

Q: And your definition is what?

A: This court's definition in *United States v. Turkette.* An association in fact is proved by a common purpose and an ongoing organization of a continuous unit. We believe all this exists here. Your Honor, if we might turn to the injury requirement . . .

Q: And the purpose to defraud does not have to coexist with the long-term operation of the unit?

A: No, it does not, Your Honor. Furthermore, Mr. Vitas has alleged the existence of a RICO injury. He has alleged that because of respondent's RICO violations, he has suffered damages in the amount of $650,000. Again, Your Honor, the language of the statute is clear. Section 1964(c) of RICO states that anyone injured by reason of a RICO violation may sue in court and shall recover treble damages. There is no limitation on the type of injury that must be alleged under RICO. We have a direct injury. $650,000 was lost because of the securities fraud.

Q: Your co-counsel seemed to indicate that in this case, the expectation of the parties was to buy and sell a business. You are not suggesting that the parties could waive their right under the Securities Acts, are you?

A: As my co-counsel indicated, if the purchasers choose to waive their rights in the Securities Acts in buying or selling a business, they would have the option of doing so by structuring it as a sale of the assets of the company, including any outstanding stock.

Q: If you buy stock, from a broker, the broker can't ask you to waive the rights of the Securities Act, can he?

A: No, Your Honor.

Q: Would it change this case at all if the sellers of the stock had asked for a stipulation that the transaction was the sale of a business, and not to be covered by the Securities Acts?

A: If they'd chosen to do that they could have sold the assets in Wholesale Computer.

Q: And if they only added an extra clause in the contract saying that this was to be considered the sale of a business?

A: They would be contractually trying to take themselves out of the protection of the Securities Act, and this should not be encouraged. If they have the option of removing themselves from those protections by structuring their sale as a sale of assets, then this message should be sent to business people by the Court.

Hdbk.App. Advocacy 2nd Ed. ACB—7

Q: Please take a moment to conclude.

A: Yes, Your Honor. Mr. Vitas has alleged all the necessary elements
     of RICO cause of action. RICO applies to all individuals equally
     and because this is a 12(b) motion, the facts in the complaint must
     be construed in a light favorable to Mr. Vitas. Mr. Vitas is entitled
     to his day in court. Thank you.

Appendix C

CHECKLISTS FOR WRITTEN BRIEF AND ORAL ARGUMENT

No matter how extensively an advocate prepares a first draft of a brief or an oral presentation, it is necessary to review the draft or presentation before it is finalized. This is the essence of effective editing. To assist the advocate in this final revision, the following checklists are provided. These checklists have been adapted from the evaluation sheets used in the UCLA Moot Court Honors Program.

WRITTEN BRIEF CHECKLIST

1. OVERALL APPEARANCE
   Are all necessary sections in the brief? _____
   Is the typing and the physical presentation neat? _____

2. COVER OF THE BRIEF
   In compliance with the rules of the proper court? _____

3. TOPICAL INDEX
   Are the sections of the brief in proper sequence? _____
   Is the overall form correct (including even right hand margins)? _____

4. TABLE OF AUTHORITIES
   Does the table contain sensible division and arrangement of statutes and secondary source material; division of federal and state cases into separate categories? _____
   Are authorities properly cited? _____
   Should an appendix have been used? Are the items in the appendix the proper type of items? Is the appendix referred to in the body of the brief or was it added as an afterthought? _____

5. WHY THIS COURT HAS JURISDICTION

    A. OPINIONS BELOW

        Does the brief inform the court of the opinions below?   _____

    B. JURISDICTION

        Does the brief contain the proper statement of jurisdiction?   _____

6. QUESTIONS PRESENTED

Are the questions phrased such that an answer favorable to the advocate is naturally suggested?   _____

Are the questions specific and tied to the facts of the case?   _____

Is the wording active and assertive?   _____

Is each question stated clearly and simply?   _____

7. STATEMENT OF THE CASE

Is the nature of case described, relieving the court of speculating or spotting the issues?   _____

Are the parties identified?   _____

Are the lower court proceedings explained?   _____

Which party is appealing from what?   _____

Is the statement worded to favor the advocate's position without being overly argumentative in tone?   _____

Are only those facts set forth which are relevant to the issues or which are needed for an understanding of the case?   _____

Do the facts persuade the reader to the position of the advocate? Are the facts structured and sequenced in the most persuasive manner? Is clarity retained as to the chronology and interrelationships of the facts? Are subheadings used where appropriate? Are the facts stated in an interesting manner? Is a non-argumentative tone maintained?   _____

8. SUMMARY OF ARGUMENT

Are the advocate's important arguments summarized in the most concise and persuasive manner?   _____

Is the wording clear and simple?   _____

Is the wording assertive and active?   _____

9. ARGUMENT

    A. GENERAL CONSIDERATIONS   _____

        Is the brief at all times persuasive?   _____

        Are the results requested shown to be factually just? Are these results wedded to arguments which are technically sound, both legally and logically?   _____

        Are all important issues addressed?   _____

Are the issues properly analyzed?   _____

Is a theme developed for the brief from the facts
which are most favorable to the advocate's position? Are any favorable facts omitted? Are any
unfavorable facts included?   _____

Is the theme of favorable facts used to tie the separate issues into one stream of logically-related
argument?   _____

Is the theme stated strongly, clearly, and positively
with no hesitation or perceptible weakness?   _____

Are the issues structured and presented in a logical
sequence? While maintaining a logical structure,
is the sequence adopted the most persuasive pat-
tern available?   _____

B. CAPTIONS

Are the captions clear, persuasive statements of
each issue? Is each worded actively and assertive-
ly? Is each caption tied into the specific facts of
the case?   _____

Does each caption make resolution of each issue in
favor of the advocate seem logical and just?   _____

Do the captions when read together in the Topical
Index provide a first-time reader with a succinct
statement of the issues of the case and with a
persuasive view of the advocate's positions on the
issues?   _____

Are subheadings needed? Are they most appropri-
ately used?   _____

C. TEXT OF ARGUMENT

Is the text easily readable? Is it concise and clear
but interesting? Is it stripped of all irrelevancies
and clutter?   _____

Is the argument low-keyed and subdued but relent-
less? Are bombast and extravagance avoided?   _____

Does each element of the argument fall logically
within the scope of the caption? Is any information present which should be set forth under a
different caption or subheading? Are thought-
interrupting footnotes only used when the information is needed and logic and continuity may
only be preserved by use of them?   _____

Is the applicable legal principle clear? Is this principle tied to specific facts of the case? Does the
combination of principle and fact persuasively sug-
gest the desired conclusion?   _____

Is case law appropriately used? For cases principally relied upon, are the facts described in sufficient detail to place the holding in the proper framework to make the brief's reliance upon it logical and persuasive? If the case is relied upon in a lesser fashion, is a parenthetical factual statement used to provide sufficient context for the reliance? _____

Is case law persuasively used? Are only appropriate, effective quotes used? Are string cites avoided where the principle is clear and established? If the principle is not clearly established but is the subject of confusion or is within a trend, are the numerous cases cited effectively used to show the case at bar to be within the holdings or trend? Is the requested result the logical product of such a showing? _____

Is overreliance on certain cases avoided even where such cases are thought to be controlling? Are helpful policy arguments brought in effectively? Are policies and facts used together to buttress the case law and to compel the court to find the case law to be controlling? _____

Are the points of the opposition anticipated and implicitly (or explicitly, where appropriate) rebutted or otherwise rendered ineffectual, irrelevant, or unpersuasive? _____

Are unfavorable precedents effectively confronted? _____

Is the overall argument sufficiently complete to enable a judge to read and absorb it without ever having to resort to looking up a cited authority or any other materials outside the record and the briefs? _____

10. CONCLUSION

Is the type of relief desired clearly requested? _____

If a Summary of Argument is part of the brief, does the Conclusion omit any resummarization of the arguments? _____

ORAL PRESENTATION CHECKLIST

I. ORGANIZATION OF THE PRESENTATION

1. INTRODUCTION

Introduce himself, his party and if appropriate, his co-counsel? _____

Are the issues to be discussed and the highlights of the argument previewed for the court? _____

2. CLARITY OF ORGANIZATION
    Are the arguments presented in logical sequence?   _____
    Are smooth transitions made from one argument to
    another?   _____
    Does the organization aid and insure clarity and
    comprehension of the various arguments?   _____

3. ALLOCATION OF TIME
    Is time allocated among arguments in an efficient
    manner?   _____
    Does the allocation of time anticipate and allot the
    most time to those specific issues which most con-
    cern the Court?   _____

4. CONCLUSION
    Does the argument conclude with a concise and
    effective summary of the major points?   _____

II. DEVELOPMENT OF THE ARGUMENT

1. PERSUASIVENESS
    Is maximum effective use made of the strongest
    points? Were weaker points made in such a way
    as to minimize any detrimental impact of such
    points?   _____
    Are the arguments presented in the most persuasive
    sequence?   _____
    Are the arguments of the opposing side anticipated
    and minimized by proper selection of available
    arguments?   _____

2. ARGUMENT SUPPORT
    Is the best case law authority used? Are the strong-
    est policy arguments made and emphasized?   _____

3. APPLICATION OF LAW TO FACTS
    Are the arguments and authorities effectively tied
    into the facts of the case?   _____
    Are cases relied on properly analyzed and used to
    support arguments or show similarity to the facts
    of the case at bar?   _____
    Is each step of the argument logical in its welding of
    facts, law and policy?   _____

III. RESPONSES TO QUESTIONS FROM THE BENCH

1. PREPARATION
    Is the speaker adequately prepared to answer all
    questions?   _____
    Are the facts and holdings of cited authorities and
    the details of policy arguments clearly recalled,
    understood, and applied?   _____

2. RESPONSIVENESS

Does the advocate answer the questions posed without first beating around the bush?   _____

Are the responses persuasive? Do they address the court's concerns and attempt to dispel those doubts with the best authority and logic possible?   _____

Do the responses evoke an empathy from the court toward the advocate's position and client?   _____

3. FLEXIBILITY

Is the advocate able to adjust his presentation to immediately address any persistent concern of the court over a specific issue?   _____

Is the advocate able to continue the presentation in an organized manner after each question is answered?   _____

4. PERCEPTION

Is the advocate able to understand the questions from the tribunal and perceive what elements the court considers troublesome or unpersuasive?   _____

IV. SPEAKING ABILITY

1. ADVOCACY

Will the advocate's speech and manner at all times convey conviction and purpose on behalf of the client? Does the advocate avoid appearing overly scholarly or detached from the client's position?   _____

2. SPEAKING TECHNIQUE

Does the advocate speak without undue hesitation and with proper diction?   _____

Are inflection and modulation used appropriately—avoiding either a monotone or a distracting overuse of inflection or modulation?   _____

Does the advocate choose appropriate words? Are bombast and extravagance avoided?   _____

3. DEMEANOR

Does the advocate appear poised and relaxed?   _____

Is composure and tact retained at all times, even under stress?   _____

Are notes avoided or used effectively—e.g., unobtrusively, without excessive reliance?   _____

Is eye contact frequent? Does it convey interest and conviction?   _____

Are gestures used appropriately—avoiding either a wooden appearance or a distracting impression of hyperactive limbs and facial muscles?   _____

4. OVERALL EFFECTIVENESS
Does the advocate's use of the above attitudes, techniques, and skills combine to make the advocate's arguments and responses to questions significantly more persuasive? Is great weight thereby added to the argument presented? ———

*

Appendix D

EXCERPTS FROM:
GUIDELINES FOR EQUAL
TREATMENT
OF THE SEXES
IN McGRAW-HILL BOOK
COMPANY PUBLICATIONS

Reprinted with permission.

GENERALLY

The following excerpts were taken from materials which were designed by the McGraw-Hill Book company to make staff members and authors aware of the ways in which males and females have been stereotyped in publications; to show the role language has played in reinforcing inequality; and to indicate positive approaches toward providing fair, accurate, and balanced treatment of both sexes in our publications. The recommendations in these guidelines are intended primarily for use in teaching materials, reference works, and nonfiction works in general.

Men and women should be treated primarily as people, and not primarily as members of opposite sexes. Their shared humanity and common attributes should be stressed—not their gender difference. Neither sex should be stereotyped or arbitrarily assigned to a leading or secondary role.

Generally, written materials should be addressed to readers of both sexes. However, when as a practical matter it is known that a writing will be used primarily by women for the life of the edition (say, the next five years), it is pointless to pretend that the readership is divided equally between males and females. In such cases it may be more beneficial to address the book fully to women and exploit every opportunity (1) to point out to them a broader set of options than they might otherwise have considered, and (2) to encourage them to aspire to a more active, assertive, and policy-making role than they might otherwise have thought of.

Women and men should be treated with the same respect, dignity, and seriousness. Neither should be trivialized or stereotyped, either in text or in illustrations. Women should not be described by physical attributes when men are being described by mental attributes or professional position. Instead, both sexes should be dealt with in the same terms. References to a man's or a woman's appearance, charm, or intuition should be avoided when irrelevant.

NO	YES
Henry Harris is a shrewd lawyer and his wife Ann is a striking brunette.	The Harrises are an attractive couple. Henry is a handsome blond and Ann is a striking brunette.
	OR The Harrises are highly respected in their fields. Ann is an accomplished musician and Henry is a shrewd lawyer.
	OR The Harrises are an interesting couple. Henry is a shrewd lawyer and Ann is very active in community (*or* church or civic) affairs.

In descriptions of women, a patronizing or girl-watching tone should be avoided, as should sexual innuendoes, jokes, and puns. Examples of practices to be avoided: focusing on physical appearance (a buxom blonde; using special female-gender word forms (poetess, aviatrix, usherette); treating women as sex objects or portraying the typical woman as weak, helpless; making women figures of fun or objects of scorn and treating their issues as humorous or unimportant.

Examples of stereotypes to be avoided: scatterbrained female, fragile flower, goddess on a pedestal, catty gossip, henpecking shrew, apron-wearing mother, frustrated spinster, ladylike little girl. Jokes at women's expense—such as the woman driver or nagging mother-in-law cliches—are to be avoided.

NO	YES
the fair sex; the weaker sex	women
the distaff side	the female side of line

the girls or the ladies (when adult females are meant)	the women
girl, as in: I'll have my girl check that.	I'll have my secretary (or my assistant) check that. (Or use the person's name.)
lady used as a modifier, as lady lawyer	lawyer (A woman may be identified simply through the choice of pronouns, as in: The lawyer made her summation to the jury. Try to avoid gender modifiers altogether. When you must
modify,	use women or female, as in: A course on women writers, or the airline's first female pilot.)
the little woman; the better half	wife
female-gender word forms, such as authoress, poetess, Jewess	author, poet, Jew
female-gender or diminutive word forms, such as suffragette, usherette, aviatrix	suffragist, usher, aviator (or pilot)
libber (put-down)	feminist; liberationist
sweet young thing	young woman; girl
co-ed (as a noun)	student

(Note: Logically, co-ed should refer to any student at a co-educational college or university. Since it does not, it is a sexist term.)

housewife	homemaker for a person who works at home, or rephrase with a more precise or more inclusive term
career girl or career woman	name the woman's profession: attorney Ellen Smith; Marie Sanchez, a journalist or editor or business executive or doctor or lawyer or agent
cleaning woman, cleaning lady, or maid	housekeeper; house or office cleaner
The sound of the drilling disturbed the housewives in the neighborhood.	The sound of the drilling disturbed everyone within earshot (or everyone in the neighborhood).

| Housewives are feeling the pinch of higher prices. | Consumers (customers or shoppers) are feeling the pinch of higher prices. |

In descriptions of men, especially men in the home, references to general ineptness should be avoided. Men should not be characterized as dependent on women for meals, or clumsy in household maintenance, or as foolish in self-care.

To be avoided: characterizations that stress men's dependence on women for advice on what to wear and what to eat, inability of men to care for themselves in times of illness, and men as objects of fun (the henpecked husband).

Women should be treated as part of the rule, not as the exception. Generic terms, such as doctor and nurse, should be assumed to include both men and women. Modified titles, such as "woman doctor" or "male nurse," should be avoided. Work should never be stereotyped as "woman's work" or as "a man-sized job." Writers should avoid showing a "gee-whiz" attitude toward women who perform competently ("Though a woman, she ran the business as well as any man" or "Though a woman, she ran the business efficiently.")

Terms such as *pioneer, farmer,* and *settler* should not be used as though they applied only to adult males.

NO	YES
Pioneers moved West, taking their wives and children with them.	Pioneer families moved West. Pioneer men and women (*or* pioneer couples) moved West, taking their children with them.

Women should not be portrayed as needing male permission in order to act or to exercise rights (except, of course, for historical or factual accuracy).

NO	YES
Jim Weiss allows his wife to work part-time.	Judy Weiss works part-time.

Women should be recognized for their own achievements. Intelligent, daring, and innovative women, both in history and in fiction, should be provided as role-models for girls, and leaders in the fight for women's rights should be honored and respected, not mocked or ignored.

LANGUAGE CONSIDERATIONS

In references to humanity at large, language should operate to include women and girls. Terms that tend to exclude females should be avoided whenever possible.

The word *man* has long been used not only to denote a person of male gender, but also generically to denote humanity at large. To many people today, however, the word *man* has become so closely associated with the first meaning (a male human being) that they consider it no longer broad enough to be applied to any person or to human beings as a whole. In deference to this position, alternative expressions should be used in place of *man* (or derivative constructions used generically to signify humanity at large) whenever such substitutions can be made without producing an awkward or artificial construction. In cases where *man*-words must be used, special efforts should be made to ensure that pictures and other devices make explicit that such references include women.

Here are some possible substitutions for *man*-words:

NO	YES
mankind	humanity, human beings, human race, people
primitive man	primitive people or peoples; primitive human beings; primitive men and women
man's achievements	human achievements
If a man drove 50 miles at 60 mph . . .	If a person (or driver) drove 50 miles at 60 mph . . .
the best man for the job	the best person (or candidate) for the job
man-made	artificial; synthetic; manufactured; constructed; of human origin
manpower	human power; human energy; workers; workforce
grow to manhood	grow to adulthood; grow to manhood or womanhood

PRONOUNS

The English language lacks a generic singular pronoun signifying *he* or *she,* and therefore it has been customary and grammatically sanctioned to use masculine pronouns in expressions such as "one . . . *he,*" "anyone . . . *he,*" and "each child opens *his* book." Nevertheless, avoid when possible the pronouns *he, him,* and *his* in reference to the hypothetical person or humanity in general.

Various alternatives may be considered:

(1) Reword to eliminate unnecessary gender pronouns;

(2) Recast in the plural;

(3) Replace the masculine pronoun with *one, you, he* or *she, her* or *his,* as appropriate. (Use *he* or *she* and its variations sparingly to avoid clumsy prose;

(4) Alternate male and female expressions and examples.

NO	YES
I've often heard supervisors say, "He's not the right man for the job," or "He lacks the qualifications for success."	I've often heard supervisors say, "She's not the right person for the job," or "He lacks the qualifications for success."

These guidelines can only suggest a few solutions to difficult problems of rewording. The proper solution in any given passage must depend on the context and on the author's intention. For example, it would be wrong to pluralize in contexts stressing a one-to-one relationship, as between teacher and child. In such cases, the expression *he or she* or either *he* or *she* as appropriate will be acceptable.

OCCUPATIONS

Occupational terms ending in *man* should be replaced whenever possible by terms than can include members of either sex unless they refer to a particular person who is in fact male. (Each occupational title suggested below is already in wide use.)

NO	YES
congressman	member of Congress; representative (but *Congressman* Koch and Congress*woman* Holtzman)
businessman	business executive; business manager
fireman	fire fighter
mailman	mail carrier; letter carrier
salesman	sales representative; salesperson; sales clerk
insurance man	insurance agent
statesman	leader; public servant
chairman	person presiding at (or chairing) a meeting; presiding officer; the chair head; leader; coordinator; moderator
cameraman	camera operator
foreman	supervisor

Language that assumes all readers are male should be avoided.

NO	YES
you and your wife	you and your spouse
when you shave in the morning	when you brush your teeth (or wash up) in the morning

PARALLEL TREATMENT

The language used to designate and describe females and males should treat the sexes equally.

Parallel language should be used for women and men.

NO	YES
the men and the ladies	the men and the women; the ladies and the gentlemen; the girls and the boys
man and wife	husband and wife

Note that *lady* and *gentlemen, wife* and *husband,* and *mother* and *father* are role words. *Ladies* should be used for women only when men are being referred to as *gentlemen.* Similarly, women should be called *wives* and *mothers* only when men are referred to as *husbands* and *fathers.* Like a male shopper, a woman in a grocery store should be called a *customer,* not a *housewife.*

NAMES

Women should be identified by their own names (e.g., Indira Gandhi). They should not be referred to in terms of their roles as wife, mother, sister, or daughter unless it is in these roles that they are significant in context. Nor should they be identified in terms of their marital relationships (Mrs. Gandhi) unless this brief form is stylistically more convenient (than, say Prime Minister Gandhi) or is paired with similar references to men.

A woman should be referred to by name in the same way that a man is. Both should be called by their full names, by first or last name only, or by title.

NO	YES
Bobby Riggs and Billie Jean	Bobby Riggs and Billie Jean King
Billie Jean and Riggs	Billie Jean and Bobby
Mrs. King and Riggs	King and Riggs
	Ms. King (because she prefers Ms.) and Mr. Riggs
Mrs. Meir and Moshe Dayan	Golda Meir and Moshe Dayan or Mrs. Meir and Dr. Dayan

Unnecessary reference to or emphasis on a woman's marital status should be avoided. Whether married or not, a woman may be referred to by the name by which she chooses to be known, whether her name is her original name or her married name.

Whenever possible, a term should be used that includes both sexes. Unnecessary references to gender should be avoided.

NO	YES
college boys and coeds	students

TITLES

Insofar as possible, job titles should be nonsexist. Different nomenclature should not be used for the same job depending on whether it is held by a male or by a female. (See page 13 for additional examples of words ending in *man*.)

NO	YES
steward or purser or stewardess	flight attendant
policeman and policewoman	police officer
maid and houseboy	house or office cleaner; servant

Different pronouns should not be linked with certain work or occupations on the assumption that the worker is always (or usually) female or male. Instead either pluralize or use *he* or *she* and *her* or *his*.

NO	YES
the consumer or shopper . . . she	consumers or shoppers . . . they
the secretary . . . she	secretaries . . . they
the breadwinner . . . his earnings	the breadwinner . . . his or her earnings or breadwinners . . . their earnings.

Males should not always be first in order of mention. Instead, alternate the order, sometimes using: women and men, gentlemen and ladies, she or he, her or his.

Index

References are to Pages.

181